interactive SCIENCE

A black bear cub's short, sharp claws help it climb trees.

PEARSON

Glenview, Illinois • Boston, Massachusetts • Chandler, Arizona • New York, New York

Authors

You are an author!

This is your own special book to keep. You can write all of your science discoveries in your book. That is why you are an author of this book.

Print your name, school, town, and state below. Then write to tell everyone all about you.

My Picture

Name

School

Town

State

All About Me

Credits appear on pages EM18–EM19, which constitute an extension of this copyright page.

On The Cover
A black bear cub's short, sharp claws help it climb trees.

ISBN-13: 978-0-328-87137-7
ISBN-10: 0-328-87137-0
4 16

Program Authors

DON BUCKLEY, M.Sc.
Director of Technology & Innovation,
The School at Columbia University, New York, New York
Don Buckley has transformed learning spaces, textbooks, and media resources so that they work for students and teachers. He has advanced degrees from leading European universities, is a former industrial chemist, published photographer, and former consultant to MOMA's Education Department. He also teaches a graduate course at Columbia Teacher's College in Educational Technology and directs the Technology and Innovation program at the school. He is passionate about travel, architecture, design, change, the future, and innovation.

ZIPPORAH MILLER, M.A.Ed.
Coordinator for K-12 Science Programs, Anne Arundel County Public Schools.
Mrs. Zipporah Miller served as a reviewer during the development of Next Generation Science Standards and provides national training to teachers, administrators, higher education staff and informal science stakeholders on the Next Generation Science Standards. Prior to her appointment in Anne Arundel, Mrs. Miller served as the Associate Executive Director for Professional Development Programs and Conferences at the National Science Teachers Association (NSTA).

MICHAEL J. PADILLA, Ph.D.
Eugene P. Moore School of Education, Clemson University, Clemson, South Carolina
A former middle school teacher and a leader in middle school science education, Dr. Michael Padilla has served as president of the National Science Teachers Association and reviewed the Next Generation Science Standards. He is a former professor of science education at Clemson University. As lead author of the *Science Explorer* series, Dr. Padilla has inspired the team in developing a program that promotes student inquiry and meets the needs of today's students.

KATHRYN THORNTON, Ph.D.
Professor, Mechanical & Aerospace Engineering, University of Virginia, Charlottesville, Virginia
Selected by NASA in May 1984, Dr. Kathryn Thornton is a veteran of four space flights. She has logged more than 975 hours in space, including more than 21 hours of extravehicular activity. As an author on the *Scott Foresman Science* series, Dr. Thornton's enthusiasm for science has inspired teachers around the globe.

MICHAEL E. WYSESSION, Ph.D.
Associate Professor of Earth and Planetary Science, Washington University, St. Louis, Missouri
An author on more than 50 scientific publications, Dr. Wysession was awarded the prestigious Packard Foundation Fellowship and Presidential Faculty Fellowship for his research in geophysics. Dr. Wysession is an expert on Earth's inner structure and has mapped various regions of Earth using seismic tomography. He is known internationally for his work in geoscience education and research, and was an author of the Next Generation Science Standards.

Instructional Design Author

GRANT WIGGINS, Ed.D.
President, Authentic Education, Hopewell, New Jersey
Dr. Wiggins is a co-author with Jay McTighe of *Understanding by Design, 2nd Edition* (ASCD 2005). His approach to instructional design provides teachers with a disciplined way of thinking about curriculum design, assessment, and instruction that moves teaching from covering content to ensuring understanding.
UNDERSTANDING BY DESIGN® and UbD™ are trademarks of ASCD, and are used under license.

Activities Author

KAREN L. OSTLUND, Ph.D.
Past President, National Science Teachers Association, Arlington, Virginia
Dr. Ostlund has over 40 years of experience teaching at the elementary, middle school, and university levels. She was Director of WINGS Online (Welcoming Interns and Novices with Guidance and Support) and the Director of the UTeach/Dell Center for New Teacher Success with the UTeach program in the College of Natural Sciences at the University of Texas at Austin. She also served as Director of the Center for Science Education at the University of Texas at Arlington, as President of the Council of Elementary Science International, and as a member of the Board of Directors of the National Science Teachers Association. As an author of Scott Foresman Science, Dr. Ostlund was instrumental in developing inquiry activities.

ELL Consultant

JIM CUMMINS, Ph.D.
Professor and Canada Research Chair, Curriculum, Teaching and Learning Department at the University of Toronto
Dr. Cummins's research focuses on literacy development in multilingual schools and the role technology plays in learning across the curriculum. *Interactive Science* incorporates research-based principles for integrating language with the teaching of academic content based on Dr. Cummins's work.

Reviewers

Program Consultants

Content Reviewers

Energy

These wind turbines use wind to make electricity.

PearsonRealize.com

Go online for engaging videos, interactivities, and virtual labs.

Chapter 2

Plants and Animals

Salamanders live part of their life in water and part on land.

PearsonRealize.com

Go online for engaging videos, interactivities, and virtual labs.

Patterns in Space

The sun warms the land, water, and air.

PearsonRealize.com

Go online for engaging videos, interactivities, and virtual labs.

The Nature of Science

This girl is collecting scientific information.

PearsonRealize.com

Go online for engaging videos, interactivities, and virtual labs.

The Design Process

This house for wood ducks is made of natural materials.

PearsonRealize.com

Go online for engaging videos, interactivities, and virtual labs.

Videos that bring Science to **life!**

Go to **PearsonRealize.com** to watch exciting Untamed Science videos!

The Untamed Science team has created a unique video for every chapter in this book!

"This is your book. You can write in it!"

interactive SCIENCE

Big Question

At the start of each chapter you will see two questions—an **Engaging Question** and a **Big Question.** Just like a scientist, you will predict an answer to the Engaging Question. Each Big Question will help you start thinking about the Big Ideas of science. Look for the symbol throughout the chapter!

How is a giraffe like a zebra?

Plants and Animals

Chapter 2

Try It! What do plants need to be healthy?

STEM Activity Trap It and Learn!

Lesson 1 What are the parts of plants?

Lesson 2 What are some kinds of animals?

Lesson 3 What are some parts of animals?

Lesson 4 Where do plants and animals live?

Lesson 5 How do living things get food?

Investigate It! How does water affect plant growth?

Life Science

Apply It! How can an octopus use its arms?

an X on two things that the ...ffe needs. **Tell** how your needs and giraffe's needs are alike.

How do plants, animal... ...d people live in their habit...

Let's Read Science!

You will see a page like this toward the beginning of each chapter. It will show you how to use a reading skill that will help you understand what you read.

Let's Read Science!

◉ Compare and Contrast
Compare means to tell how things are alike. **Contrast** means to tell how things are different.

Whales and Fish
Whales and fish live in the ocean. Fish get oxygen from the water. Whales must come to the surface to breathe. Whales get oxygen from the air, like you.

This Southern Right Whale is coming up for air ▽

Practice It!
Compare and **contrast** whales and fish.

Compare	Contrast

PearsonRealize.com   65

Vocabulary Smart Cards

inquiry
observe
tool
conclusion
hypothesis
data

conclusion
conclusión

inquiry
indagación

Play a Game!

Cut out the cards.

Work with a partner.

One person puts the cards picture side up.

The other person puts the cards picture side down.

Work together to match each word with its meaning.

199

hypothesis
hipótesis

observe
observar

data
datos

tool
instrumento

Vocabulary Smart Cards

Go to the end of the chapter and cut out your own set of **Vocabulary Smart Cards.** Draw a picture to learn the word. Play a game with a classmate to practice using the word!

PearsonRealize.com

Go to **PearsonRealize.com** for a variety of digital activities.

interactive SCIENCE

Envision It!

At the beginning of each lesson, at the top of the page, you will see an **Envision It!** interactivity that gives you the opportunity to circle, draw, write, or respond to the Envision It! question.

Lesson 4
How do some animals grow?

Envision It!

Draw how the pig will look when it is grown.

I will know how some animals grow and change.

Word to Know
nymph

MY PLANET DIARY **Fact or Fiction?**

Read Together

All eggs from birds are the same, right? No, eggs can be very different. Think about eggs you get from the store. They are mostly the same size and color. These eggs come from chickens. Ostrich eggs are as big as a grapefruit. They are the biggest eggs in the world. Robin eggs are often blue. Quail eggs can be speckled.

Tell how the ostrich egg and the robin egg are alike and different.

quail egg

robin egg

ostrich egg

Animal Life Cycles

Animals have life cycles.
A life cycle is the way a living thing grows and changes.

A goat is an animal.
A baby goat looks like its parents.
The baby goat grows and changes.
A grown goat may have young of its own.
The life cycle begins again.

Number the goats in the order of their life cycle.

72

MY PLANET DIARY

My Planet Diary will introduce you to amazing scientists, fun facts, and important discoveries in science. They will also help you to overcome common misconceptions about science concepts.

Read See DO!

After reading small chunks of information, stop to check your understanding. The visuals help teach about what you read. Answer questions, underline text, draw pictures, or label models.

Gases

Gas is matter that does not have its own size or shape. Gas takes the size and shape of what it is in. Gas takes up all of the space inside its container. The bubbles in the picture are filled with gas.

You know that air is all around you. Air is made of gases that you cannot see.

How are liquids and gases alike?

Draw an arrow to the gas in a bubble.

Tell what shape the gas takes.

Where is the gas in this bouncer?

Do the math!

Tally

You can use tally marks to record information.

This is a tally mark. |

These are 5 tally marks. ||||

This chart shows how many living things are in the picture.

Living Things	Tally	Total
Tree			1
Bird		
Lizard		

Write tally marks to record how many birds and lizards are in the picture. Then write the totals.

Find one more living thing in the picture. **Record** the information in the chart.

Scientists commonly use math as a tool to help them answer science questions. You can practice skills that you are learning in math class right in your *Interactive Science* Student Edition!

Got it?

At the end of each chapter you will have a chance to evaluate your own progress! At this point you can stop or go on to the next chapter.

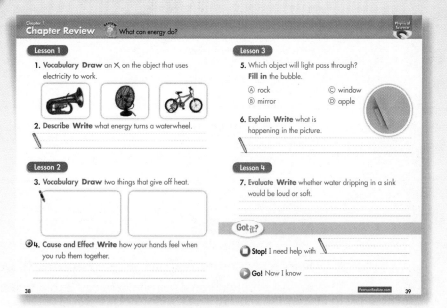

Chapter Review — What can energy do?

Lesson 1

1. Vocabulary **Draw** an X on the object that uses electricity to work.

2. Describe **Write** what energy turns a waterwheel.

Lesson 2

3. Vocabulary **Draw** two things that give off heat.

4. Cause and Effect **Write** how your hands feel when you rub them together.

Lesson 3

5. Which object will light pass through? **Fill in** the bubble.
   - Ⓐ rock
   - Ⓑ mirror
   - Ⓒ window
   - Ⓓ apple

6. Explain **Write** what is happening in the picture.

Lesson 4

7. Evaluate **Write** whether water dripping in a sink would be loud or soft.

Got it?

Stop! I need help with

Go! Now I know

"Have fun! Be a scientist!"

interactive SCIENCE

Try It!

At the start of every chapter, you will have the chance to do a hands-on inquiry activity. The activity will provide you with experiences that will prepare you for the chapter lessons or may raise a new question in your mind.

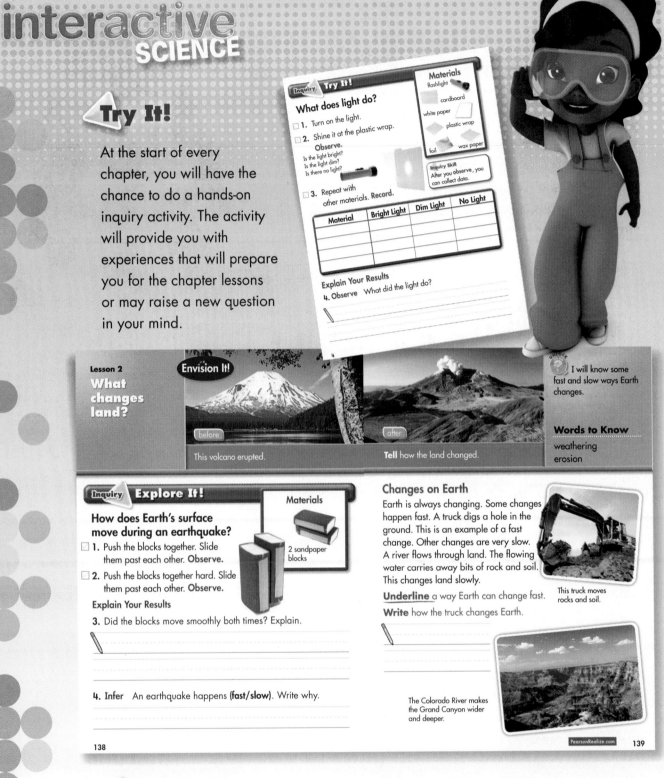

Inquiry Try It!

What does light do?

☐ 1. Turn on the light.

☐ 2. Shine it at the plastic wrap.
   Observe.
   Is the light bright?
   Is the light dim?
   Is there no light?

☐ 3. Repeat with other materials. Record.

Material	Bright Light	Dim Light	No Light

Explain Your Results
4. **Observe** What did the light do?

Materials
flashlight
cardboard
white paper
plastic wrap
foil   wax paper

Inquiry Skill
After you observe, you can collect data.

Lesson 2
What changes land?

Envision It!

before — This volcano erupted.

after — **Tell** how the land changed.

I will know some fast and slow ways Earth changes.

Words to Know
weathering
erosion

Inquiry Explore It!

How does Earth's surface move during an earthquake?

☐ 1. Push the blocks together. Slide them past each other. **Observe.**

☐ 2. Push the blocks together hard. Slide them past each other. **Observe.**

Explain Your Results

3. Did the blocks move smoothly both times? Explain.

4. **Infer** An earthquake happens (**fast/slow**). Write why.

Materials
2 sandpaper blocks

Changes on Earth

Earth is always changing. Some changes happen fast. A truck digs a hole in the ground. This is an example of a fast change. Other changes are very slow. A river flows through land. The flowing water carries away bits of rock and soil. This changes land slowly.

Underline a way Earth can change fast.

Write how the truck changes Earth.

This truck moves rocks and soil.

The Colorado River makes the Grand Canyon wider and deeper.

PearsonRealize.com

138   139

Explore It!

Before you start reading the lesson, **Explore It!** activities provide you with an opportunity to first explore the content!

Design It!

The **Design It!** activity has you use the engineering design process to find solutions to problems. By finding a problem and then planning, drawing, and choosing materials, you will make, test, and evaluate a solution for a real world problem. Communicate your evidence through drawings and prototypes and identify ways to make your solution better.

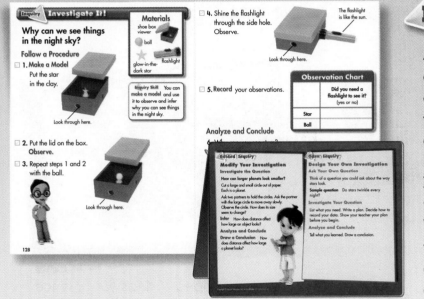

Investigate It!

At the end of every chapter, a Directed Inquiry activity gives you a chance to put together everything you've learned in the chapter. Using the activity card, apply design principles in the Guided version to Modify Your Investigation or the Open version to Develop Your Own Investigation. Whether you need a lot of support from your teacher or you're ready to explore on your own, there are fun hands-on activities that match your interests.

Apply It!

These Open Inquiry activities give you a chance to plan and carry out investigations.

What is Pearson Realize?

Interactive Science is now part of Pearson's brand-new learning management system, Realize! With rich and engaging content, embedded assessment with instant data, and flexible classroom management tools, Realize gives you the power to raise interest and achievement for every student in your classroom.

Engaging Videos

Engage with science topics through videos! Start each chapter with an Untamed Science video.

Pearson Flipped Videos for Science give you another way to learn.

Interactivities and Virtual Labs

Practice science content with engaging online activities.

At **PearsonRealize.com** go online and conduct labs virtually! No goggles and no mess.

Connect to What You Know

Check what you know at the end of each lesson and chapter.

Get More Practice on skills and content, based on your performance.

Predict your exam readiness with benchmark assessments.

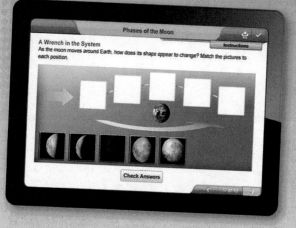

Pearson Realize offers powerful classroom management functionality, including:

Standards-aligned content — search by standard

Powerful Search tools — search by keyword, topic or standards

Customizable curriculum — reorder the table of contents, uploadfiles and media, add links and create custom lessons and assessments

Flexible class management tools — create classes, organize students, and create assignments targeted to students, groups of students, or the entire class.

Tracks student progress — instantly access student and class data that shows standards mastery on assessments, online activity and overall progress.

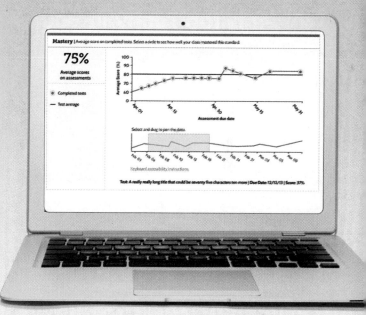

Track Your Learning Online.

PearsonRealize.com

STEM Quest

Keep Out the Sun!

Your Quest is to make a curtain.
Your cat ripped the curtain!
Now it is too sunny in your room.

You will make a model curtain.
Test how much light your curtain blocks.

Quest Kick-Off
Keep Out the Sun!
Watch a video about light.
How many types of light are there?

Quest Check-In 1
Light and Sight
Find out about light.
How does light change color?
How does light change details?

Quest Check-In 2
Blocking Light
Do a lab.
Shine light on materials to make images.

Quest Check-In 3
How We Use Light
Learn how we communicate with light.

Quest Findings
Design a Curtain
Build a window frame.
Test your curtain.
Change your curtain!

What makes food cook on a grill?

Energy

Tell what you know about the coals in the grill.

 What can energy do?

What does light do?

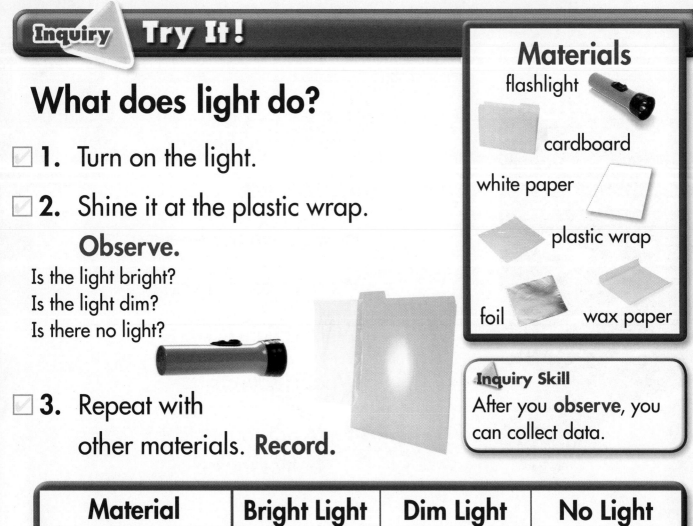

Materials
flashlight

cardboard

white paper

plastic wrap

foil   wax paper

☐ **1.** Turn on the light.

☐ **2.** Shine it at the plastic wrap.

Observe.
Is the light bright?
Is the light dim?
Is there no light?

☐ **3.** Repeat with
other materials. **Record.**

Inquiry Skill
After you **observe**, you can collect data.

Material	Bright Light	Dim Light	No Light

Explain Your Results

4. Observe What did the light do?

_____

_____

_____

◉ Cause and Effect

A **cause** is why something happens.

An **effect** is what happens.

A Windy Day

It is a windy day.
You run across the park.
You hold your kite high.
The wind catches it.
Soon the kite flies in the sky!

Practice It!

Write what happens when the wind catches a kite.

Cause

The wind catches the kite.

Effect

Let's Talk!

People talk on the phone every day. When have you talked on the phone? Who did you talk to?

Some phones are connected by wire. The wire connects your phone to another phone. You speak into a phone. The person on the other phone can hear your voice. Most phones are not connected by wire. Signals travel through the air from one phone to another. All kinds of phones let people talk over a distance.

You can make another kind of phone. It is called a string phone.
Discover how you can send messages by connecting objects.

Find a Problem

☑ **1.** You are standing on one side of the room. Your partner is standing on the other. You need a way to tell your partner something important. What can you build?

☑ **2. Draw** what you will build.

Plan and Draw

☑ **3.** Where does sound come from? What happens when an object vibrates?

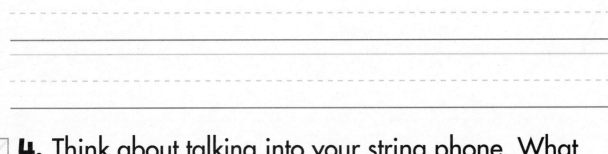

☑ **4.** Think about talking into your string phone. What parts of the string phone will vibrate? **Draw**.

5. How long will the string be?

6. How will you attach your cup to the string?

Choose Materials

Look at the materials. Think about how to make a string phone.

☑ **7.** Talk with your partner about ways you might use the materials.

☑ **8.** What could make your design difficult?

_____

_____

_____

_____

☑ **9.** What is one material you will not choose. Write why.

_____

_____

_____

_____

☐ **10. Draw** what your string phone will look like. **Draw** yourself and your partner using the string phone. **Label** all of the materials.

Make and Test

☐ **11.** Work with your partner to build your string phone.

☐ **12.** **Draw** your string phone after you build it.
Does it look the same as your plan? Does it look
different from your plan? Write.

☑ **13.** **Test** your string phone. Does it work? Can your partner hear you? Can you hear your partner? Write what you hear.

☑ **14.** Take two steps closer to your partner. **Test** your string phone again. Does it work as well as before? Write what you hear.

Record and Share

☐ **15. Compare** your string phone with another string phone. How are the two string phones the same?

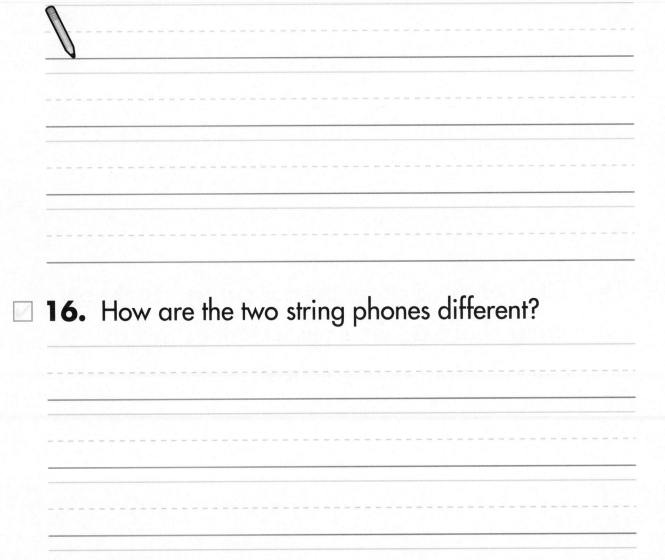

☐ **16.** How are the two string phones different?

17. How can you change your string phone to make it better?

18. Draw your new design. **Label** all of the materials.

How do we use energy?

Tell what things in the picture use energy.

my planet Diary Did You Know?

Read Together

We can use the wind to make electricity. Look at the picture. The machines are wind turbines. A wind turbine is like a giant pinwheel. The wind turns the turbine's blades. The turning blades move parts inside the turbine. These parts make electricity.

Could the turbines make electricity if the wind was not blowing? Why?

_____

_____

_____

Words to Know

electricity

energy

Energy

Click! You turn on the lamp.

Electricity makes the lamp glow.

The lamp will not glow without electricity.

Electricity is a kind of energy.

Energy can cause change or do work.

◎ **Cause and Effect Write** what happens if you turn off electricity to the lamp.

The lamp glows. It lets you see things near it.

Cause

The lamp has no electricity.

Effect

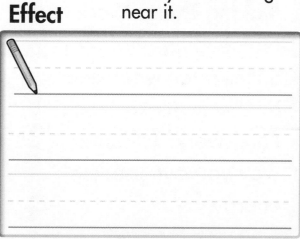

Cars and Energy

Cars use energy.

Most cars get energy from fuel.
Some fuel is burned to make
heat or power.

Cars use gasoline for fuel.
A car's engine burns the gasoline.
The car has energy to move.

Tell what gives the car in the picture
the energy to move.

Cars get gasoline from
gas pumps.

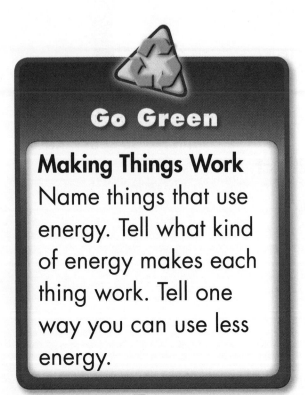

Go Green

Making Things Work
Name things that use
energy. Tell what kind
of energy makes each
thing work. Tell one
way you can use less
energy.

Using Energy

Moving water has energy.
Moving water turns the waterwheel in the picture.

Batteries store energy.
Batteries change the stored energy to electricity.
The toy car uses electricity to move.

Wind the key.
The robot stores energy as you wind.
Let go of the key.
The robot moves.
The stored energy changes to moving energy.

Tell where the waterwheel gets energy to move.

Write where each object gets energy.

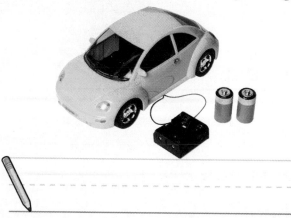

Lesson 2

What gives off heat?

Draw an X on what makes heat.

Explore It!

How can texture affect the heat produced by rubbing?

☐ **1.** Rub 2 plastic squares together for 10 seconds. Feel them. **Record.**

☐ **2.** Repeat using the sandpaper squares.

Explain Your Results

3. Which material felt warmer? Explain.

4. Infer Does rubbing rougher materials together produce more or less heat?

Materials

2 sandpaper squares

2 plastic squares

clock with second hand

20

Heat from Sunlight

Heat comes from the sun.

Heat moves from warmer places to cooler places.

Heat moves from warmer objects to cooler objects.

Sunlight warms the land.

Sunlight warms the water.

Sunlight warms the air.

The sand is warmer on a sunny day than on a cloudy day.

◉ **Cause and Effect**

Write what warms the sand at the beach.

_____

_____

Heat from People

Heat comes from people.
Rub your hands together fast.
How do your hands feel?
Your hands feel warm.
Rubbing your hands together
makes heat.
Running makes heat too.

Tell how the children in the
picture make heat.

◉ **Cause and Effect** How can you
make heat with your hands?

You make heat when
you move.
You can feel the heat
when you run.

Lightning Lab

Make Heat
Run in place. Keep
running for two
minutes. How do you
feel? Tell a partner.

22

Heat from Fire

Look at the picture above.
Heat comes from the fire.
The heat warms the food.
The heat warms the air.

Draw arrows on the picture
to show how heat is moving.
List two other things that can
give off heat.

_____

_____

What is light?

Draw one more object that makes light.

my planet Diary INVENTION!

The first electric lights did not last long. They would burn out quickly. Thomas Edison wanted a light that lasted a long time. Thomas Edison and his team worked hard. They found a material that did not burn out quickly. They used the material to make the light bulb.

Write why light bulbs are important.

_____

_____

_____

Word to Know

shadow

What Makes Light

Light is a kind of energy.

We can see light energy.

Light comes from the sun.

Light comes from other stars.

Light comes from candles.

Light comes from lamps too.

Circle where light might come from.

Look at the pictures.

Tell two more things that make light.

Fireflies give off their own light. We can see fireflies at night.

Light Shines Through

Light passes through a window.
Light passes through thin paper.
Light will not pass through you.
You make a shadow.

A **shadow** forms when
something blocks the light.

Tell why you can see the light in
the lanterns.

Draw a picture of you and
your shadow.

26

What Light Can Do

Light travels in a straight line.
Light bounces off objects that
are smooth and shiny.
Light bounces back to you from
a mirror.
That is why you can see yourself.

◎ **Cause and Effect** Look at the
pictures. **Tell** how the shape of the
mirror changes what you see.

Lesson 4

What is sound?

Tell about the sounds these instruments make.

Inquiry Explore It!

How can you make sound?

☐ **1. Measure** 2 meters of string.

☐ **2.** Tie the string tight around a desk.

☐ **3.** Pluck the string.

Put the blocks under the string.

☐ **4.** Tell what happened when you plucked the string.

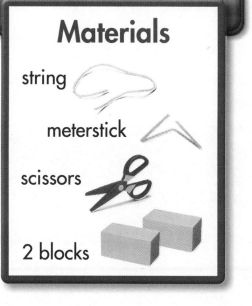

Materials

string

meterstick

scissors

2 blocks

Explain Your Results

5. Communicate How can you change the sound?

28

Word to Know

vibrate

Sounds

Sound is a kind of energy.

We can hear sound energy.

Sound comes from objects that vibrate.

Vibrate means to move back and forth very fast.

The boy plucks the guitar strings.

You hear sound when the strings vibrate.

You hear sound when you talk on the phone.

Signals travel through the air from one phone to another.

Phones let you talk to someone far away.

Different guitar strings make different sounds.

◉ **Cause and Effect** Tap your pencil on your desk. **Tell** what happens.

Loud and Soft

Listen to the sounds around you.

Some sounds are loud.

Some sounds are soft.

A school bell ringing is loud.

The chirp of a baby bird is soft.

Circle the picture below that shows something that makes a loud sound.

Draw an X on what makes a soft sound.

High and Low

Some sounds are high.
Some sounds are low.
You can sing a song in
a high voice.
You can sing a song in
a low voice.

(Circle) the picture that shows
something that makes
a low sound.

At-Home Lab

Making Sounds
Use different objects
to make sounds. List
the sounds in a chart.
Write if each sound is
high or low. Write if
each sound is loud
or soft.

What sounds can bottles make?

Follow a Procedure

☐ **1.** Blow over the top of Bottle A. Listen to the sound.

☐ **2.** Repeat Step 1 with Bottle B and Bottle C.

Materials

2 bottles with water

1 almost empty bottle

Inquiry Skill
When you **infer**, you figure something out.

☑ **3. Record** the sounds you hear.

Sounds from Each Bottle	
Bottle	**Sound**
A (almost empty)	
B (half full)	
C (almost full)	

Analyze and Conclude

4. Write a sentence about each sound.

5. Infer   How did the bottles make sounds?

Solar Power

The sun can help us make electricity. Look at the car and the house. Find the panels. These are called solar panels. Solar panels collect energy from the sun. The panels turn the energy into electricity. Solar power helps keep the air clean. This helps the environment.

Underline what solar panels do.
Circle the solar panels on the house.
Tell what is making the car work.

Vocabulary Smart Cards

- electricity
- energy
- heat
- shadow
- vibrate

Play a Game!

Cut out the cards.

Work with a partner.

Pick a card.

Show your partner the front of the card.

Have your partner make a sentence about the word.

35

shadow

sombra

electricity

electricidad

vibrate

vibrar

energy

energía

heat

calor

energy that makes
lamps and other
things work

energía que hace
que las lámparas
y otros objetos
funcionen

dark shape made
when something
blocks light

forma oscura que se
forma cuando algo
bloquea la luz

something that can
cause change or do
work

algo que puede
causar un cambio
o hacer que algo
funcione

to move back and
forth very fast

mover hacia delante
y hacia atrás muy
rápidamente

moves from warmer
places to cooler
places

se mueve de lugares
más cálidos a lugares
más fríos

Lesson 1
How is energy used?
- We use energy to make things work.
- Electricity and gasoline are kinds of energy.

Lesson 2
What gives off heat?
- Heat moves from warmer to cooler places.
- The sun and people give off heat.

Lesson 3
What is light?
- Light passes through some things.
- A shadow is made when light is blocked.

Lesson 4
What is sound?
- Sounds are made when things vibrate.
- Sounds can be loud or soft or high or low.

Chapter Review

Lesson 1

1. **Vocabulary Draw** an X on the object that uses electricity to work.

2. **Describe Write** what energy turns a waterwheel.

_____

- -

Lesson 2

3. **Vocabulary Draw** two things that give off heat.

4. **Cause and Effect Write** how your hands feel when you rub them together.

_____

- -

_____

Lesson 3

5. Which object will light pass through?
   Fill in the bubble.

   Ⓐ rock   Ⓒ window

   Ⓑ mirror   Ⓓ apple

6. **Explain Write** what is
   happening in the picture.

   -

Lesson 4

7. **Evaluate Write** whether water dripping in a sink
   would be loud or soft.

   -

   -

Got it?

⬛ **Stop!** I need help with _____

   -

▶ **Go!** Now I know _____

How does light move through water?

Materials

flashlight

plastic cup

plastic bottle with water

milk

plastic spoon

construction paper

ruler

> **Inquiry Skill** In an **experiment** you test a question you have.

Ask a question.

What happens as light moves through water?

Make a prediction.

1. If water is not clear, light will move through it (a) a lot, (b) a little, (c) not at all. Predict.

_____

Plan a fair test.

Use the same setup each time.

Design your test.

☐ **2.** Draw how you will set up your test.

☐ **3.** List your steps.

_____

_____

_____

_____

Do your test.

☑ **4.** Follow your steps.

Collect and record data.

☑ **5.** Fill in the chart.

Tell your conclusion.

6. When did the most and least light get through?

_____

_____

7. **Infer** What blocked the light off?

_____

_____

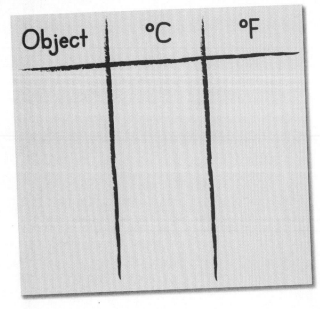

Record Temperature

- Use a thermometer to find the temperature of different objects.
- Measure temperature in Celsius (°C) and Fahrenheit (°F).
- Record your findings in a chart.

Create an Exhibit

- An exhibit is a display.
- Show sources of energy you use at home, school, and play.

Science and Engineering Practices

1. Ask a question or define a problem.
2. Develop and use models.
3. Plan and carry out investigations.
4. Analyze and interpret data.
5. Use math and computational thinking.
6. Construct explanations or design solutions.
7. Engage in argument from evidence.
8. Obtain, evaluate, and communicate information.

Make a Presentation

- Use a flashlight to make shadows of your hand.
- Make the shadows different shapes.
- Tell why the shadows form.

Send a Message with Sound

- Work with a partner. Use patterns of pencil taps to stand for certain letters or words.
- List the tap patterns and the letters or words.
- Think of a simple message to send by tapping the pencil.
- Tap the message and see if your partner can tell it to you. Switch roles.

How is a young orangutan like its mother?

Plants and Animals

Try It! How are flowers alike and different?

STEM Activity Mix It Up!

Lesson 1 What are some groups of living things?

Lesson 2 What are some parts of plants?

Lesson 3 How do plants grow?

Lesson 4 How do some animals grow?

Lesson 5 How are living things like their parents?

Lesson 6 How are groups of living things different?

Investigate It! How do different seeds grow?

Life Science

Apply It! How can a mouse's color help keep it safe from hawks?

Tell one way the baby and its mother are alike.

 THE BIG How are living things alike and different?

How are flowers alike and different?

☐ **1.** Take a flower apart.

☐ **2. Classify** Group the parts that are alike.

Materials

hand lens

paper

different flowers

Inquiry Skill
Classify means to sort things into groups that are alike and different.

☐ **3. Observe** Compare the parts that are different.

Explain Your Results

4. Communicate How are the parts alike?

_____

_____

5. How are the parts different?

_____

_____

_____

_____

Compare and Contrast

You **compare** when you tell
how things are alike.
You **contrast** when you tell
how things are different.

Two Kinds of Bears

Grizzly bears live in North America.
Pandas live in Asia.
Both bears have fur.
One bear has brown fur.
The other bear has black
and white fur.

grizzly bear

panda

Practice It!

Write how the grizzly bear and panda are alike
and different.

Compare	Contrast

Mix It Up!

Plants need nutrients to grow. Plants get nutrients from soil. People can add nutrients to soil to help plants grow. Compost is a mixture of food scraps and dead plants. Food scraps and plants break down in a compost pile. Compost has a lot of nutrients. Nutrients make soil rich. You can make a compost pile. You will choose materials. You will see how to make rich soil.

Find out what rots in a compost pile.

Find out what those things need to rot.

Write what you discover.

Find a Problem

☐ **1.** You need rich soil to grow plants. What will you do to make soil rich?

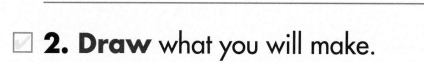

☑ **2. Draw** what you will make.

Plan and Draw

Think about your compost pile. Where will it be? Circle your choices.

☑ **3.** My compost pile will be:

    in shade   in sun   in part shade and sun

☑ **4.** Write why.

_____

_____

_____

☑ **5.** My compost pile will be:

    in the classroom   in the school yard

☑ **6.** Write why.

_____

_____

_____

☑ **7. Draw** where your compost pile will be.

Choose Materials

Look at the materials. Think about how to make a compost pile.

☑ **8.** What could make your design difficult?

_____

_____

_____

_____

☑ **9.** Pick one material you will not use. Write why.

_____

_____

_____

_____

☑ **10. Draw** what your compost pile will look like. **Label** the things you will put in the pile.

Make and Test

☐ **11.** Make your compost pile. **Observe** it each week. **Record** changes you see.

Week	Compost Pile Observation
1	
2	
3	
4	
5	

☐ **12. Draw** the materials in the compost pile.
Write how they look.

Record and Share

☑ **13. Compare** your compost pile with another group's compost. How are the compost piles the same?

☑ **14.** How are the compost piles different?

☐ **15.** How will you change your plan?

_____

_____

_____

☐ **16.** How will the compost pile look different? **Draw**.

What are some groups of living things?

Envision It!

Tell one way you can group the animals in the pictures.

MY PLANET DIARY

Did You Know?

Read Together

What do you think this picture shows?

It lives underwater. It is a group of animals. It can be many different, beautiful colors. Groups of this make up reefs near coastlines.

Do you know what it is yet? It is coral.

The coral in the picture is called brain coral.

Why do you think it has that name?

Word to Know

backbone

Groups of Living Things

Plants and animals are living things. You can group living things in different ways.

You can group living things by size. You can group living things by color. You can group living things by shape. Scientists group living things too.

⊙ **Compare and Contrast Write** how the cardinal and the betta fish are alike and different.

cardinal

betta

Compare	Contrast

Plants With Flowers

There are two main plant groups. One group of plants grows flowers. The other group of plants does not grow flowers.

Plants with flowers make seeds. Seeds grow in the flowers. Plants with flowers grow in many places.

Draw a plant that grows flowers.

At-Home Lab

Plant Groups

Collect pictures of plants. Work with an adult. Group the pictures. One group should be plants that grow flowers. The other group should be plants that do not grow flowers.

Flowers grow on some trees.

Plants Without Flowers

Some plants do not have flowers.

Some plants have cones.

Seeds grow inside the cones.

Some plants do not have flowers or cones.

These plants do not make any seeds.

These plants often grow in wet places.

(Circle) the plants that make seeds.

Name two plants that do not grow flowers.

Pine trees have cones.

This moss does not make seeds.

Animal Groups

One group of animals has backbones.
A **backbone** is the set of bones along
the middle of the back.
Mammals are animals with backbones.
Most mammals have fur or hair.

moose

Birds have backbones.
Birds are covered with feathers.
Birds have wings.

oriole

Fish have backbones.
Fish live in water.
Fish have scales.

rockfish

Match each animal with an animal group.

Animal	Group
robin	bird
hamster	fish
goldfish	mammal

Reptiles have backbones.
Most reptiles have dry skin.
Reptiles have scales.

turtle

Amphibians have backbones.
Amphibians have smooth, wet skin.

salamander

Another group of animals does not have backbones.
This is the largest group of animals.
Insects are part of this group.
All insects have six legs.

ant

(Circle) the insect.

What are some parts of plants?

Tell what plant parts you see.

my planet diary Did You Know?

Most of the ground in the tundra is frozen. Do you think plants will grow in the tundra?

_____

_____

Only a few inches of soil in the tundra are not frozen. Plant roots need space to grow underground. Some plants without roots can grow in the tundra. Mosses are plants. Mosses do not have roots. Mosses can grow in the tundra.

Do you think trees with long roots grow in the tundra? Explain.

_____

_____

Draw the missing tulip parts.

UNLOCK
THE BIG
? I will know some parts of plants and what the parts do.

Words to Know

root   stem
leaf

Parts of Plants

Plants have different parts.
The parts help the plant live and grow.
The parts help the plant get what
it needs.

An iris and a tulip are plants.
They have the same parts.
They do not look alike.

iris

⊙ **Compare and Contrast Write** how the
iris and the tulip are alike and different.

Compare

Contrast

Roots, Stems, and Leaves

Many plants have roots.

Roots hold the plant in the ground.

Roots take in water.

Many plants have leaves and stems too.

The **stem** takes water from the roots
to other parts of the plant.

The **leaf** makes food for the plant.

Draw arrows to show how
water will move inside the plant.

leaf

flower

roots

stem

Flowers and Fruit

Many plants have flowers.
Seeds come from flowers.
Fruits come from flowers too.
Fruits have seeds.

Circle the part of the rose plant where seeds come from.

Draw a line from the word to the plant part on the rose.

(roots)　(stem)　(flowers)　(leaves)

Lightning Lab

Grow a Plant
Get a cup of dirt. Put a few seeds in it. Put the cup in a warm and sunny area. Water the seeds every day. Tell others what parts of your plant are growing.

Lesson 3

How do plants grow?

Tell what you know about seeds and plants.

Inquiry **Explore It!**

How does a seed grow?

☐ **1.** Put the seeds and towel in a bag. Seal. Put in a warm place.

☐ **2. Observe** every other day. **Record**.

Materials

6 pinto bean seeds on a wet paper towel

resealable plastic bag

hand lens

Day 1	
Day 3	
Day 5	
Day 7	

Explain Your Results

3. Predict what will happen next.

_____

68

Words to Know

life cycle
seedling

Seeds to Trees

The way a living thing grows and changes is called a **life cycle.**

An oak seed is called an acorn.
Plant an acorn in the ground.
An oak seedling grows.
A **seedling** is a very young plant.

An oak seedling has a thin stem.
An oak seedling has small leaves.
The seedling grows into a tall tree.

Draw a line from the label to the picture.

grown oak tree

oak seedling

oak seed

Life Cycle of a Plant

A seedling grows from the seed.
Roots grow downward.
A stem grows upward.
The plant grows into an
adult plant.
Some plants make flowers.
The flowers make seeds
inside fruits.
The seeds may grow into a new
plant.
The life cycle starts again.

Tell how the pepper plant grows.

⊙ **Draw Conclusions**
What might happen if a
seed did not get water?

The life cycle starts with a pepper seed.

Inside the peppers are the plant's seeds.
The seeds may grow into new plants.

A seedling grows. It has roots and a stem.

Go Green

Helpful Houseplants
Plants need air to make food. Some plants clean the air as they make food. Discuss why this is good for people and pets.

The seedling grows into an adult plant. The plant grows flowers.

The flowers grow peppers. Peppers are the plant's fruit.

How do some animals grow?

Envision It!

Draw how the pig will look when it is grown.

my planet diary

Fact or Fiction?

Read Together

All eggs from birds are the same, right? No, eggs can be very different. Think about eggs you get from the store. They are mostly the same size and color. These eggs come from chickens. Ostrich eggs are as big as a grapefruit. They are the biggest eggs in the world. Robin eggs are often blue. Quail eggs can be speckled.

Tell how the ostrich egg and the robin egg are alike and different.

quail egg

robin egg

ostrich egg

Word to Know

nymph

Animal Life Cycles

Animals have life cycles.
A life cycle is the way a living thing grows and changes.

A goat is an animal.
A baby goat looks like its parents.
The baby goat grows and changes.
A grown goat may have young of its own.
The life cycle begins again.

Number the goats in the order of their life cycle.

Life Cycle of a Sea Turtle

A sea turtle is an animal.

A sea turtle starts life as an egg.

Soon the baby sea turtle is ready to hatch.

The baby sea turtle comes out of the egg.

The sea turtle crawls to the sea and swims away from shore.

This action helps the sea turtle survive.

Underline an action that helps baby sea turtles survive.

sea turtle eggs

grown sea turtle

A baby sea turtle looks like its parents.
The sea turtle grows and changes.
Sea turtles can grow to be very big.
Grown sea turtles may have young
of their own.
The life cycle begins again.

baby sea turtle

young sea turtle

Draw arrows to show the
life cycle of the sea turtle.

Life Cycle of a Grasshopper

A grasshopper is an animal.
A grasshopper starts life as an egg.

The young grasshopper hatches.
A young grasshopper is called a nymph.
A **nymph** is a kind of young insect.
Nymphs look like their parents.
Nymphs do not have wings.

grasshopper nymph

grasshopper eggs

Circle the dragonfly nymph. **Tell** how you know it is a nymph.

76

A grown grasshopper has wings.
Grown grasshoppers may have
young of their own.
The life cycle begins again.

◉ **Compare and Contrast**

Write how a grown grasshopper
is different from a nymph.

_____

_____

_____

grown grasshopper

How are living things like their parents?

Envision It!

Tell how the animals are alike and different.

Inquiry **Explore It!**

How are babies and parents alike and different?

☐ **1.** Look at the pictures.
Talk about what you **observe.**

☐ **2. Classify** Play baby bingo.
Match the parent with its baby.

Materials

baby bingo card

bingo chips

Baby Bingo Card

Explain Your Results

3. Communicate Which babies look like their parents?

List the babies that do not look like their parents.

UNLOCK THE BIG ? I will know that plants and animals look like their parents.

Word to Know

parent

Plants and Their Parents

A **parent** is a living thing
that has young.
Plants and their parents are alike.
Plants and their parents can have
the same leaf shape.

Plants and their parents are
different too.
Plants and their parents
can have different
colored flowers.

Draw a line from
the young plant to
its parent.

young plant

How Animals and Their Parents Are Alike

Young animals are like their parents.

Many animals look like their parents.

Many animals have the same shape as their parents.

Animals and their parents can have the same number of legs.

Underline one way young animals and their parents can be alike.

Draw what the lizard's parent might look like.

The dog and its parent have the same shape.

How Animals and Their Parents Are Different

Young animals and their parents are different too.

Young animals and their parents can be different colors.

Young animals are smaller than their parents.

⊙ **Compare and Contrast**

Write how the young chickens are different from their parent.

At-Home Lab

Parents and Young
Find a picture of an animal and its young. Glue it to a sheet of paper. Write how your animals are alike and different.

The cat and its kitten are different colors.

Lesson 6

How are groups of living things different?

Color the daisy.

Inquiry **Explore It!**

How are bodies different?

☐ **1.** Have a partner trace your left foot. Use the Footprint Sheet.

☐ **2.** Put your footprint on the wall. Your teacher will tell you where.

☐ **3. Observe** all the feet.

Explain Your Results

4. Draw a Conclusion
How are the feet alike and different?

Materials

tape
(whole class use)

Footprint Sheet

_____

_____

_____

Word to Know

herd

Kinds of Plants

Plants live all around the world.
Plants of one kind are alike.
Petunias are a kind of plant.
Petunias all have fuzzy, green leaves.
Plants of one kind are different too.
Look at the pictures.
One petunia plant has pink flowers.
The other petunia plant has purple flowers.

◎ **Compare and Contrast**

Tell how petunias are alike.

Write how these petunias are different.

Kinds of Animals

Animals of one kind are alike.

Giraffes are a kind of animal.

The picture shows a herd of giraffes.

A **herd** is a group of animals of one kind
that stays together.

Giraffes have four legs and two eyes.

Giraffes have spots too.

Underline one way giraffes are alike.

Draw another giraffe in the herd.

84

Different Animals of One Kind

Animals of one kind are different too.

Some giraffes have darker spots than others.

Some giraffes have longer necks than others.

Giraffes with longer necks can reach

leaves on tall trees.

Short giraffes cannot reach as high.

Fill in the words **long**, **spots**, and **short**.

Across

1. ____ giraffes cannot reach as high.

Down

2. ___ necks help giraffes reach leaves.

3. _____on some giraffes are darker.

Lightning Lab

Alike and Different

Find two of the same kind of plant or animal. Tell how they are alike. Tell how they are different.

How do different seeds grow?

Follow a Procedure

☑ **1.** Fold a paper towel.
Put it inside a cup.

☑ **2.** Ball up another paper towel.
Put it inside the same cup.

☑ **3.** Wet the paper towels with water.

☑ **4.** Put the bean seeds in the cup.

Materials

cups

bean seeds

radish seeds

water (whole class use)

daisy seeds

paper towels

Seed Growth Chart

Inquiry Skill
You use a chart to help **collect data.**

 Be careful! Wash your hands when you finish.

☐ **5.** Repeat the steps with radish seeds.
Repeat the steps with daisy seeds.

☐ **6. Observe** the seeds for 10 days.
Collect Data Draw what you see.
Use the Seed Growth Chart.

Analyze and Conclude

7. How did the different seeds grow the same?
How did the seeds grow differently?

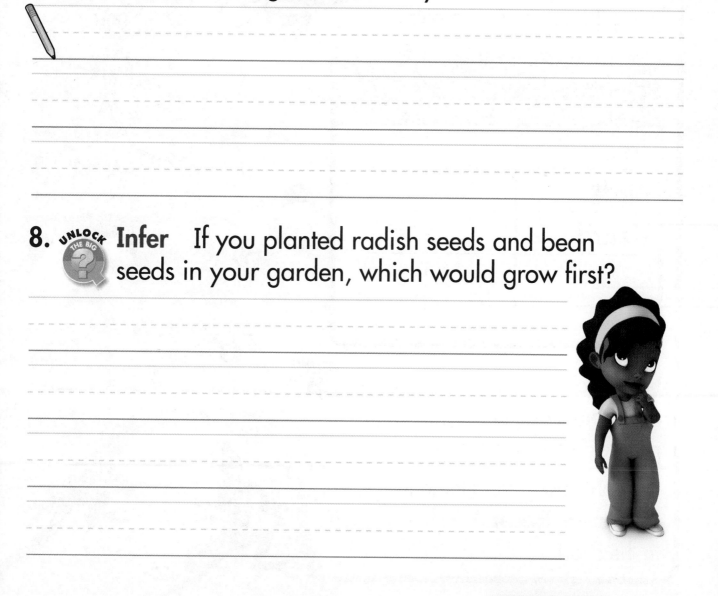

8. **Infer** If you planted radish seeds and bean seeds in your garden, which would grow first?

Do the math!
Tally

You can use tally marks to record information.

This is a tally mark. |

These are 5 tally marks. ||||

This chart shows how many living things are in the picture.

Living Things	Tally	Total
Tree			1
Bird		
Lizard		

Write tally marks to record how many birds and lizards are in the picture. Then write the totals.

Find one more living thing in the picture. **Record** the information in the chart.

Vocabulary Smart Cards

backbone
root
stem
leaf
life cycle
seedling
nymph
parent
herd

Play a Game!

Cut out the cards.

Work with a partner. Put the cards word side up.

Have your partner put the cards word side down.

Work together to match the word with the definition.

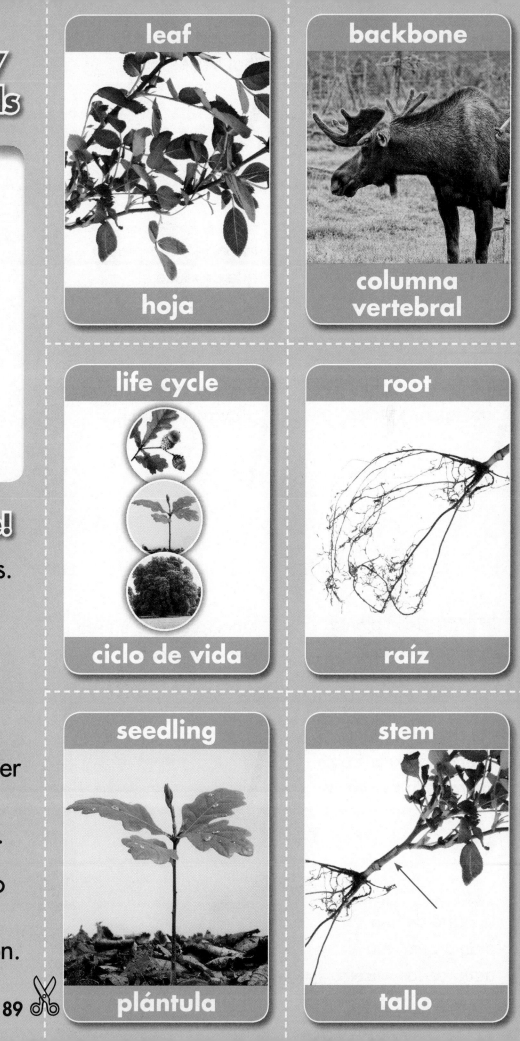

leaf

hoja

backbone

columna vertebral

life cycle

ciclo de vida

root

raíz

seedling

plántula

stem

tallo

the set of bones along the middle of the back

conjunto de huesos a lo largo del centro de la espalda

the part of a plant that makes food

la parte de la planta que produce el alimento

the part of a plant that takes in water

la parte de la planta que toma el agua

the way a living thing grows and changes

manera en que un ser vivo crece y cambia

the part of a plant that takes water from the roots to the leaves

la parte de una planta que lleva el agua de las raíces a las hojas

a very young plant

planta muy joven

90

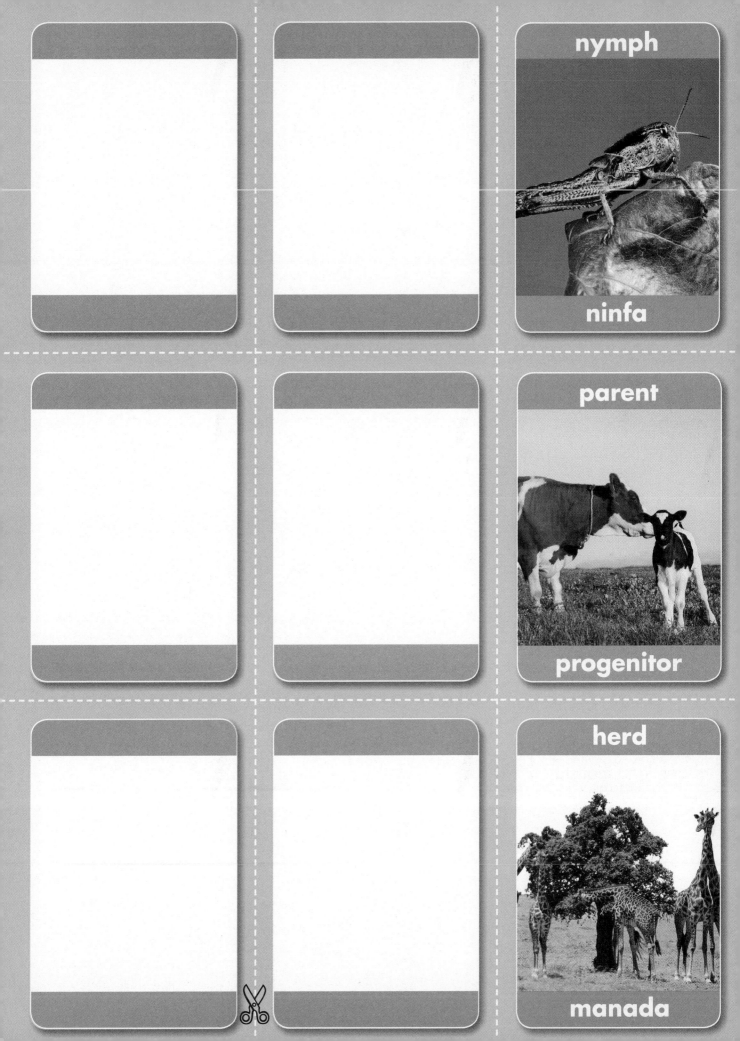

nymph

ninfa

parent

progenitor

herd

manada

a kind of young
insect

tipo de insecto joven

a living thing that has
young

ser vivo que tiene
crías

a group of animals
of one kind that stay
together

grupo de animales
del mismo tipo que
están juntos

Chapter 2
Study Guide

REVIEW THE BIG ? How are living things alike and different?

Life Science

Lesson 1

What are some groups of living things?
- One group of plants has flowers.
- One group of animals has backbones.

Lesson 2

What are some parts of plants?
- Roots and stems help plants get water.
- Leaves make food for the plant.

Lesson 3

How do plants grow?
- Plants change during their life cycle.
- A seedling is a very young plant.

Lesson 4

How do some animals grow?
- Animals change during their life cycle.
- A young grasshopper is called a nymph.

Lesson 5

How are living things like their parents?
- Parents and young can be the same shape.
- Parents and young can be different colors.

Lesson 6

How are groups of living things different?
- One kind of flower can be different colors.
- Animals in a herd are alike and different.

Lesson 1

1. Identify Write two examples of plants that make seeds.

_____

2. Which group of animals has fur or hair?
Fill in the bubble.

    Ⓐ mammals   Ⓑ birds

    Ⓒ reptiles   Ⓓ insects

Lesson 2

3. Vocabulary Label the parts of the plant.

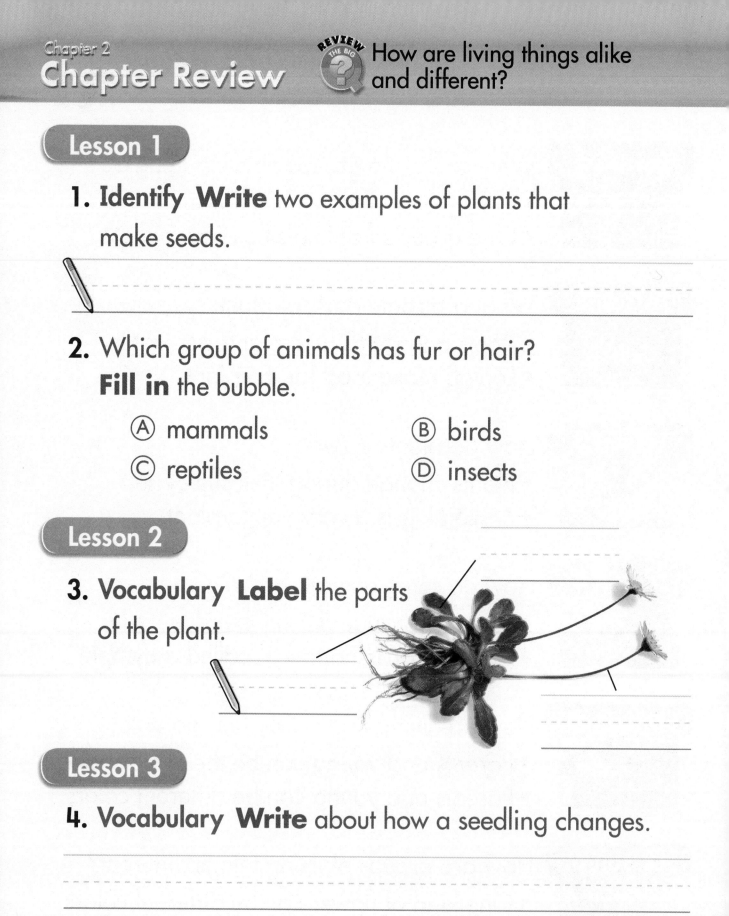

Lesson 3

4. Vocabulary Write about how a seedling changes.

_____

_____

Lesson 4

5. Apply **Draw** a
grown grasshopper.

Lesson 5

6. **Compare and Contrast** How is a young dog different
from its parents?

_____

Lesson 6

7. **Describe** How does a longer neck help a giraffe?

_____

_____

Got it?

■ **Stop!** I need help with _____

_____

▶ **Go!** Now I know _____

How can a mouse's color help keep it safe from hawks?

white beans = field where mice live
white beans with spots = light mice
black beans = dark mice

Materials

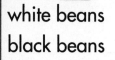

white beans

black beans

white beans with black spots

paper plate

clock with second hand (or timer or stopwatch)

Inquiry Skill
You plan an **experiment** when you design a way to answer a scientific question.

Ask a question.

How can a mouse's color help keep it safe from hunting hawks?

Make a prediction.

1. Will light-colored mice or dark-colored mice be easier to see in a field?

(a) light-colored mice

(b) dark-colored mice

Plan a fair test.

Use the same number of white beans with spots and black beans.

Design your test.

☐ **2.** List your steps.

Do your test.

☑ **3.** Follow your steps.

Collect and record data.

☑ **4.** Fill in the chart.

Tell your conclusion.

5. Which mice in your model were harder to see?

6. Infer Which mice are harder to see in a light habitat?

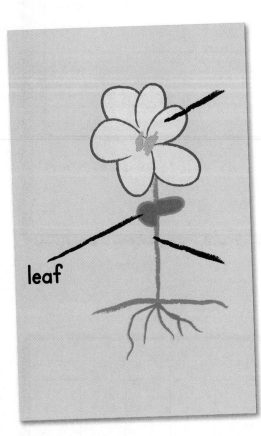

leaf

Draw a Picture

- Draw a picture of a plant.
- Show and label the parts of the plant.
- Tell how the plant changes over its life cycle.

Grow plants

- Gather soil and sand.
- Find out if plants grow better in soil or in sand.
- Use science practices.

Science and Engineering Practices

1. Ask a question or define a problem.
2. Develop and use models.
3. Plan and carry out investigations.
4. Analyze and interpret data.
5. Use math and computational thinking.
6. Construct explanations or design solutions.
7. Engage in argument from evidence.
8. Obtain, evaluate, and communicate information.

Write a Poem

- Choose an animal.

- Write a poem about what the animal needs.

- Draw a picture to go with your poem.

Design a Helmet

- Look at pictures of plants and animals that have a hard covering like the one shown.

- Use these pictures to help you design a bicycle helmet.

- Draw a picture of your helmet.

- What materials would you use to build your helmet?

- Write how it is like parts of plants and animals.

What would Earth be like without the sun?

Patterns in Space

Try It! How does the sun's movement cause shadows to change?

STEM Activity How Does a Greenhouse Work?

Lesson 1 What is the sun?

Lesson 2 What causes day and night?

Lesson 3 What are the four seasons?

Investigate It! Why can we see things in the night sky?

Earth Science

Apply It! Does the sun warm land or water faster?

Tell what Earth would be like without the sun.

? **Why is the sun important?**

How does the sun's movement cause shadows to change?

☑ **1.** Glue the Sun Tracker to cardboard.

☑ **2.** Put a piece of clay on the Sun Tracker. Put a stir stick in the clay.

☑ **3.** Put the Sun Tracker outside in the sun.

Materials

Sun Tracker

Sun Tracker

cardboard   clay

straw   glue

Inquiry Skill
You **collect data** when you mark what you observe.

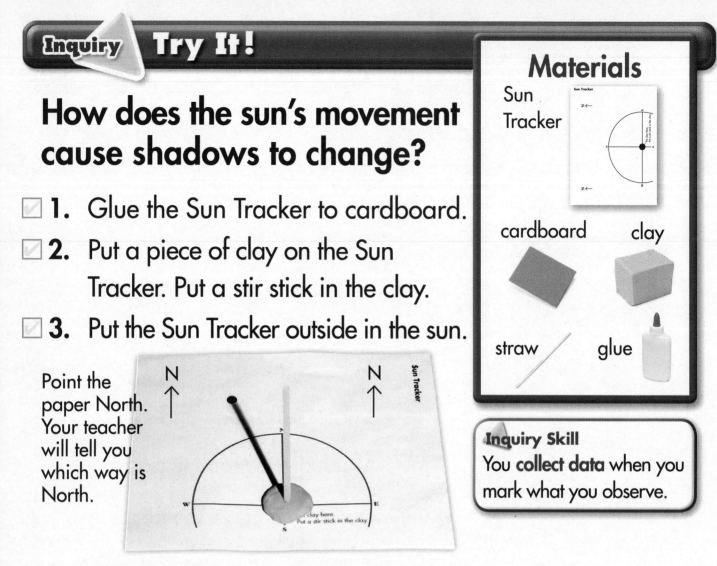

Point the paper North. Your teacher will tell you which way is North.

☑ **4.** **Observe** the tip of the shadow. Mark the tip with a dot every hour. Write the time.

☑ **5.** How did the pattern of dots change?

Explain Your Results

6. Infer How can you use a shadow to predict the sun's position?

Picture Clues

Pictures can give you **clues** about what you read.

Sunlight

You can see the sun in the sky. It shines brightly. We get light from the sun. Light from the sun warms Earth.

Practice It!

Look at the picture. **Write** how you know sunlight can melt snow.

Sunlight can melt snow.

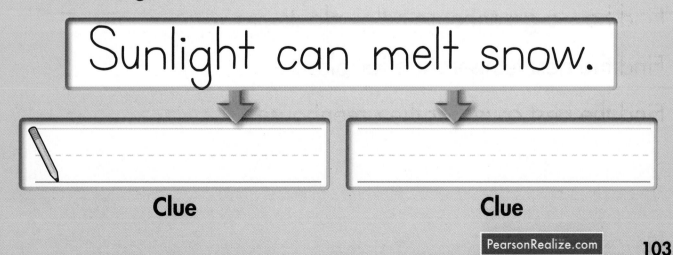

Clue   Clue

How Does a Greenhouse Work?

A greenhouse is a building. A greenhouse has glass walls. A greenhouse lets in sunlight. Sunlight helps plants grow. Plants can grow in a greenhouse. You can build a greenhouse. You will choose materials. You will build your greenhouse. You will grow a plant in your greenhouse.

Find how a greenhouse helps plants grow.

Find the best temperature for plants.

Find the best cover for the greenhouse.

Find a Problem

☑ **1.** You need a place to grow plants. It is too cold to grow plants outside. Write what you will build and why.

☑ **2. Draw** what you will build.

Plan and Draw

☑ **3.** What do plants need to grow?

☑ **4.** What plant will you grow in your greenhouse? Why?

☑ **5. Draw** a picture of the plant you will grow in your greenhouse.

Choose Materials

Look at the materials. Think about how to make a greenhouse.

☑ **6.** Talk with a partner about ways you might use the materials.

☑ **7.** What could make your design difficult?

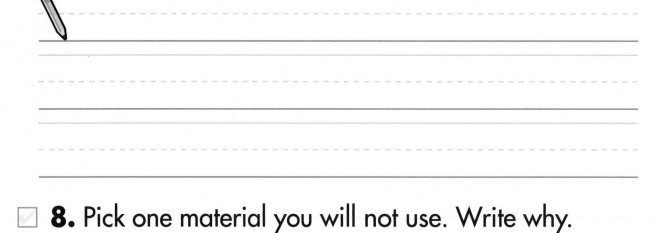

_____

_____

_____

_____

☑ **8.** Pick one material you will not use. Write why.

_____

_____

_____

_____

_____

☐ **9. Draw** what your greenhouse will look like.

Make and Test

☑ **10. Build** your greenhouse.

☑ **11. Draw** your greenhouse. Does your greenhouse look like a house? **Explain.**

☐ **12. Draw** the plants in your greenhouse. **Describe** how they grew.

Record and Share

☐ **13. Compare** your greenhouse with another greenhouse. How are the greenhouses alike?

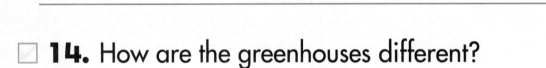

_____

_____

_____

_____

_____

☐ **14.** How are the greenhouses different?

_____

_____

_____

_____

☐ **15.** How will you change your plan?

_____

☐ **16. Draw** how your greenhouse will be different.

What is the sun?

Circle what the sun warms.

my planet Diary INVENTION!

Scientists use telescopes to observe the night sky. The first telescope was invented by Hans Lippershey. Hans Lippershey invented the telescope over 400 years ago. Newer telescopes can help you see things in more detail. People have made many discoveries using telescopes.

Write what you would observe with a telescope.

_____

UNLOCK THE BIG ? I will know ways the sun helps and harms things on Earth.

Word to Know

sun

The Nearest Star

A star is a big ball of hot gas.
The sun is a star.
The **sun** is the star that
is nearest to Earth.
The sun is bigger
than Earth.
The sun looks small
because it is far away.
You can see the sun
in the day sky.

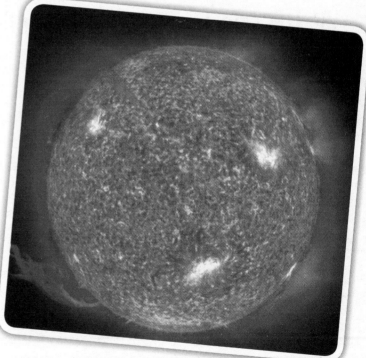

The sun is very hot
and bright.

◉ **Cause and Effect**

⟨Circle⟩ the words that tell
why the sun looks small.

Why We Need the Sun

The sun helps us.

The sun warms the land.

The sun warms the water.

The sun warms the air.

Living things need heat from the sun.

The sun lights Earth.

Plants need light from the sun to grow.

We use light from the sun to see.

Write one reason why living things need the sun.

The sun makes the day sky bright.

Out in the Sun

The sun can harm us too.
It is important to be careful
in the sun.
Too much sun can hurt your
skin and eyes.
Sunscreen and a hat can
protect you from the sun.
Some sunglasses can protect
your eyes from the sun.
You should never look
at the sun.

Underline one way the
sun harms us.

Circle two things that
protect these children
from the sun.

Lightning Lab

Heat from the Sun
Get two pieces of
clay. Put one piece in
sunlight. Put the other
in shade. Wait 10
minutes. Write how
each feels.

What causes day and night?

Tell how day and night are different.

Explore It!

How does the shape of the moon appear to change?

☑ **1.** Use a Moon Calendar.

☐ **2.** Observe the moon every night.

☐ **3. Record data** by drawing pictures on the calendar.

Materials

Moon Calendar Sheet

marker

Explain Your Results

4. Communicate Describe how the moon appears to change.

Day Sky

The sun is in the day sky.

The sun makes the day sky bright.

You may see clouds in the day sky.

You may see birds in the day sky.

Sometimes you can see the moon

in the day sky too.

day sky

Write about the day sky in the picture.

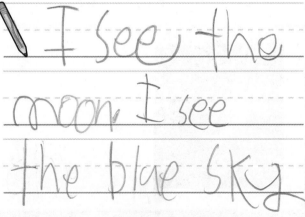

I see the moon. I see the blue sky

The moon and stars are in the night sky.
You may see clouds in the night sky.
You may see birds in the night sky too.

night sky

Circle the things that can be in the night sky.

Moon

The moon moves around Earth.
Light from the sun shines on the moon.
You only see the part of the moon lit
by the sun.
The moon looks a little different
each night.
The moon looks the same again
about every 29 days.

Draw the different ways the
moon might look.

Changes in the Sky

Observe the sky when the sun rises. Observe the sky when the sun sets. Tell your family about what you see. Never look directly at the sun.

Sunrise and Sunset

The sun seems to rise each day. The sky becomes light. The sun seems to move across the sky during the day. The sun seems to set at night. The sky becomes dark.

Tell how the sky changes from day to night.

Day and Night

The sun looks like it is moving but it is not. Earth is moving. Earth spins around and around. One spin around is called a **rotation.** Earth makes one rotation every day.

Earth is always spinning.

It is day when your part of Earth faces toward the sun. It is night when your part of Earth faces away from the sun. The rotation of Earth causes day and night.

Write what causes day and night.

_____

_____

_____

What are the four seasons?

Circle the picture that looks most like the season outside now.

my pLaneT DiaRY

Fact or Fiction?

Read Together

Suppose it is winter where you live. You may think that it is winter everywhere. It is not. People in the south half of the world are out swimming at the beach. It is summer there. The seasons in the south half of the world are opposite the seasons in the north half.

Suppose it is spring where you live. **Write** what season it is in the south half of the world.

_____

UNLOCK THE BIG ?
I will know how weather changes from season to season.

Word to Know

season

Spring

A **season** is a time of year.
The four seasons are spring,
summer, fall, and winter.
Spring comes after winter.
Spring is warmer than winter.
Daylight begins to last longer
in spring.
The sun rises earlier than in winter.
The sun sets later than in winter.
Days might be rainy.
This helps plants grow.
Many animals have babies in spring.

⊙**Sequence Write** what season
comes after winter.

_____

Alligators lay their
eggs in the spring.

Summer and Fall

Summer comes after spring.

Summer is warmer than spring.

Summer can be very dry.

Daylight lasts longest in summer.

Many plants grow in the summer.

Baby animals grow in the summer.

Fall comes after summer.

Fall is cooler than summer.

Daylight begins to shorten in fall.

Some leaves change colors.

Some animals store food for winter.

Point to the summer picture.

Point to the fall picture.

Compare summer and fall where you live.

Write how summer and fall are alike.

Vocabulary Smart Cards

sun

rotation

season

Play a Game!

Cut out the cards.

Choose a card and give your partner clues.

Have your partner guess the word.

sun

sol

rotation

rotación

season

estación

a big ball of hot gas

bala muy grande de
gas caliente

one spin around

dar una vuelta sobre
sí mismo

a time of year

período del año

Study Guide

REVIEW THE BIG ? Why is the sun important?

Lesson 1

What is the sun?
- The sun warms and lights Earth.
- The sun can harm your skin and eyes.

Lesson 2

What causes day and night?
- The sun makes the day sky bright.
- The rotation of Earth causes day and night.

Lesson 3

What are the four seasons?
- The four seasons are spring, summer, fall, and winter.

Chapter Review

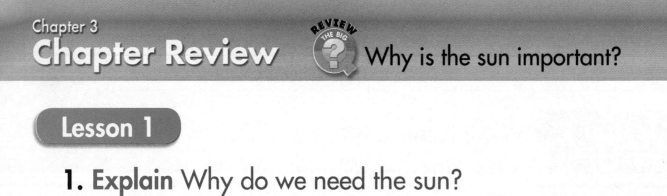

Why is the sun important?

Lesson 1

1. Explain Why do we need the sun?

2. Identify Draw two things that can protect you from the sun.

Lesson 2

3. What is NOT seen in the night sky? **Fill in** the bubble.

Ⓐ birds   Ⓒ clouds

Ⓑ moon   Ⓓ sun

4. Apply Write about what causes day and night.

Lesson 3

⊙ **5. Picture Clues Draw** an X on the picture that shows what the tree looks like in spring.

6. Describe Write what fall is like where you live.

_____

Got it?

☐ **Stop!** I need help with _____

_____

▶ **Go!** Now I know _____

Does the sun warm land or water faster?

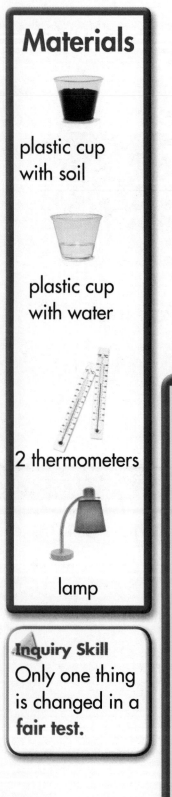

Materials

plastic cup with soil

plastic cup with water

2 thermometers

lamp

Ask a question.

Does sunlight warm soil or water faster?

Make a prediction.

1. Does soil or water warm faster in sunlight?

(a) soil

(b) water

Plan a fair test.

Use the same amount of soil and water.

Give both cups the same amount of light.

Design your test.

☐ **2.** Draw how you will set up your test.

☑ **3.** List your steps.

_____

- - - - - - - - - - - - - -

_____

- - - - - - - - - - - - - -

_____

Do your test.

☐ **4.** Follow your steps.

Collect and record data.

☑ **5.** Fill in the chart.

Tell your conclusion.

6. Which warmed faster, the cup of soil or the cup of water?

_____

- - - - - - - - - - - - - -

7. Infer Do you think the sun warms land or water faster?

_____

- - - - - - - - - - - - - -

Make a Concept Map

- Cut out pictures of the four seasons in magazines.

- Make a concept map using words and your pictures.

- Tell what weather is like in each season where you live.

Write a Song

- Write a song about the sun.

- Tell how the sun can help people.

- Tell how the sun can hurt people.

Science and Engineering Practices

1. Ask a question or define a problem.

2. Develop and use models.

3. Plan and carry out investigations.

4. Analyze and interpret data.

5. Use math and computational thinking.

6. Construct explanations or design solutions.

7. Engage in argument from evidence.

8. Obtain, evaluate, and communicate information.

Day and Night

- Use a globe.
- Mark your area on the globe with tape.
- Use a flashlight for the sun. Shine the flashlight on the globe.
- Turn the globe slowly from left to right.
- Stop the globe to show when it is daytime where you live.
- Stop the globe to show when it is nighttime where you live.

Sunrise, Sunset

- Choose a date from each season.
- Find out the time of sunrise and sunset for each date.
- Record your findings in a chart.
- Write about how sunrise time changed.
- Write about how sunset time changed.

	Sunrise Time	Sunset Time
Spring date		
Summer date		
Fall date		
Winter date		

How are you a scientist when you bake?

The Nature of Science

Circle a tool bakers use.

THE BIG **What is science?**

How do you use your senses to identify objects?

Scientists observe to find out about objects.

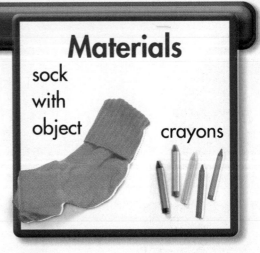

Materials

sock with object   crayons

☐ **1. Observe**   Feel the object in the sock. Do not look!

Inquiry Skill   You can use what you observe to help you **infer.**

☐ **2. Record** what it feels like.

☐ **3. Infer**   Draw the object.

Explain Your Results

4. Look at the object.
What do you see that you did not feel?

⊙ **Picture Clues**

Pictures can give you **clues** about what you read.

At the Vet

The dog is at the vet.
The vet helps the dog stay healthy.

Practice It!

Look for clues in the picture. **Write** how you know the dog stays healthy.

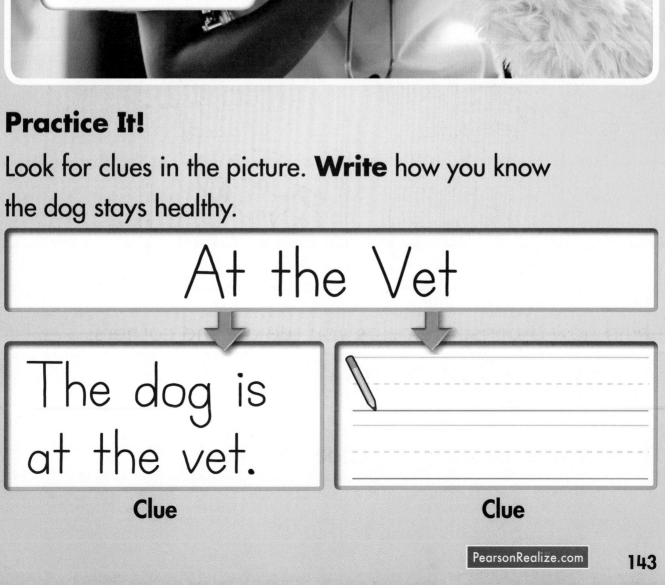

At the Vet

The dog is at the vet.

Clue

Clue

What's Over the Wall?

Light travels in a straight line. You see objects straight in front of your eyes.

Can you see over a wall or around a corner? You can with the right tool. Mirrors bounce or reflect light. A periscope is a tool that uses mirrors. You can use a periscope to see around corners. You look in one end. You see something around the corner. Underwater boats called submarines use periscopes to see what is above the water.

Find how a periscope helps you see around corners.

Find the best angle for the mirrors.

How wide should the periscope be?

Find a Problem

☑ **1.** You are on one side of a fence. Your friend is on the other. You need a tool to see your friend over the fence. What should you build?

☑ **2. Draw** what you will build.

Plan and Draw

☑ **3.** How does light travel? Write your answer. **Draw** an example.

☑ **4.** What happens when light hits a mirror at an angle? Write your answer. **Draw** an example.

☐ **5. Draw** how you can use two mirrors to change where the light will go. Show the mirrors at an angle. **Draw** where the beam of light will go.

Choose Materials

Look at the materials. Think about how to make a periscope. Think about how to bounce light so you can see over a fence.

☑ **6.** Talk with a partner. Tell how you could use each material. **Draw** the materials you will use.

☑ **7.** What could make your design difficult?

☑ **8.** What is one material you will not choose? Write why.

☐ **9. Draw** what your periscope will look like. **Draw** yourself using your periscope on one side of a fence. **Draw** your friend on the other side.

Make and Test

☐ **10.** Work with your partner to build a periscope. Think about how to put the pieces together to make them work.

☐ **11.** **Test** your periscope. Does it work? Can you see around a corner or over a fence? Write what you see.

☑ **12. Draw** your periscope. Does it look different from your plan? Write.

Record and Share

☑ **13. Compare** your periscope with another periscope. How are the periscopes alike?

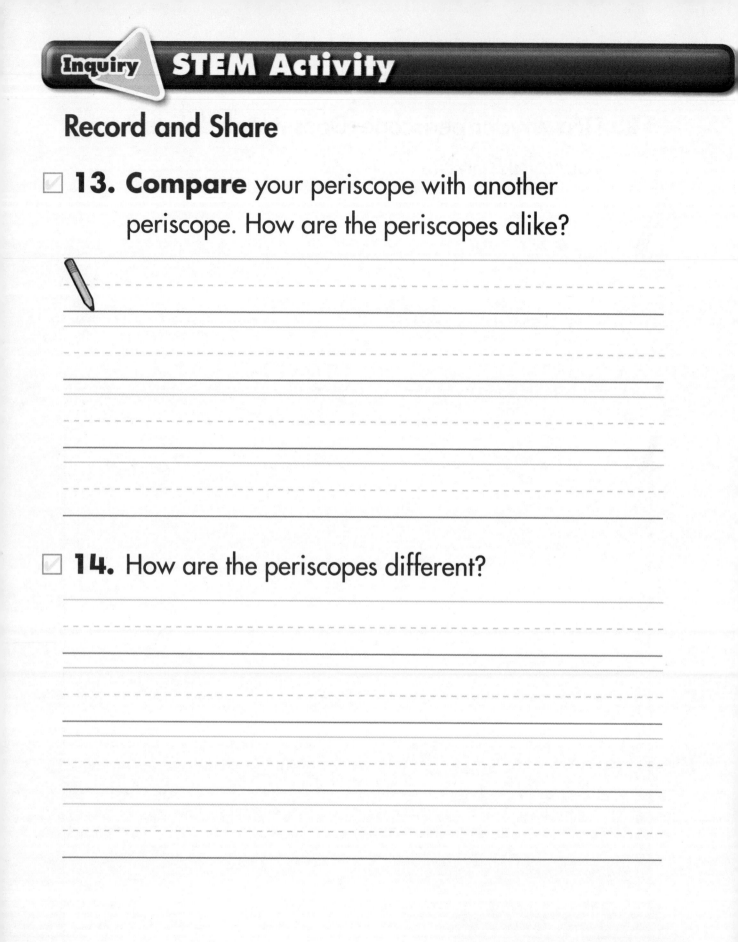

☑ **14.** How are the periscopes different?

☐ **15.** How would you change your plan?

_____

_____

_____

_____

☐ **16. Draw** a new plan. List new materials you might use.

_____

_____

_____

_____

_____

What questions do scientists ask?

Tell what a scientist might ask about the leaves.

MY PLANET DIARY DISCOVERY

Read Together

George Washington Carver discovered new ways to make things with plant parts. He made ink, shampoo, soap, paper, and rubber from peanuts!

Sometimes people like George Washington Carver are looking for new things. Sometimes people discover new things by accident. Discoveries help people do things they could not do before.

Circle one thing George Washington Carver made in a new way.

Write how you use this discovery.

_____

Scientists

Scientists are people who study the world around them.

Scientists ask and answer questions.

Scientists use inquiry.

Inquiry means looking for answers.

⊙ **Picture Clues** **Write** two questions the boy in the picture might ask.

The boy is a scientist. He is studying what is in the jar.

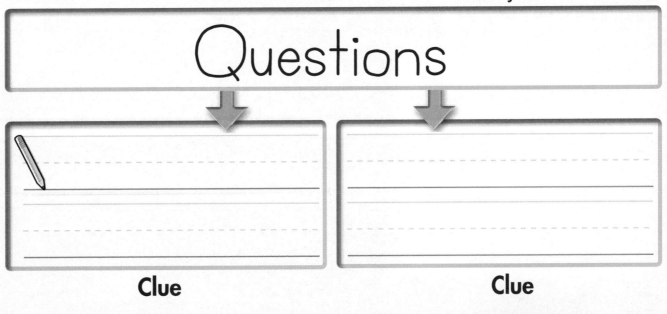

Questions

Clue

Clue

Questions

Scientists ask questions about many things.

Scientists ask questions about animals.

Scientists ask questions about plants.

Scientists ask questions about rocks
and soil.

Scientists ask questions about weather too.

Write a question you might ask about
this storm.

_____

Lightning Lab

Science Questions
Work with a partner.
Make a list of science
questions about plants
or rocks. Talk about
why the questions are
science questions.

Discovery

Scientists make discoveries.

A discovery is a new thing or idea.

Discoveries can change our lives.

The discovery of germs changed
the way people act.

Doctors did not always wash their hands
with soap.

People would get germs from the doctor.

Now doctors wash their hands with soap.

The soap gets rid of germs.

Their tools are washed with soap too.

Doctors do not pass germs to others.

Name one discovery. **Tell** how it
helped people.

What skills do scientists use?

Tell about the picture. Use your senses.

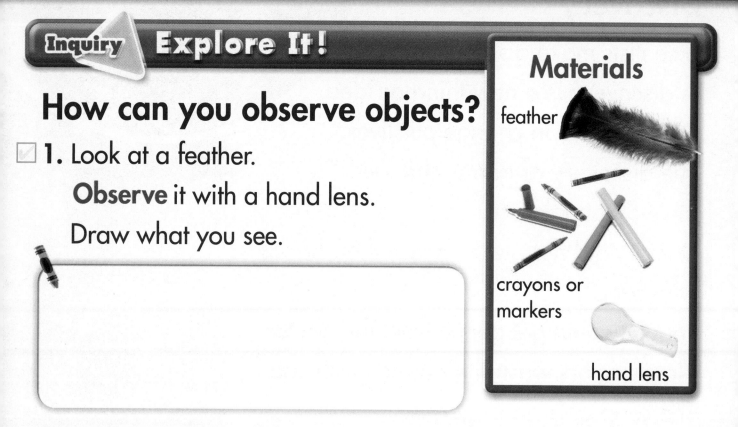

Inquiry **Explore It!**

How can you observe objects?

☑ **1.** Look at a feather.

Observe it with a hand lens.

Draw what you see.

Materials

feather

crayons or markers

hand lens

☑ **2.** Feel the feather. Tell what you learn.

Explain Your Results

3. How did the hand lens help you **observe**?

UNLOCK
THE BIG
?

I will know skills scientists use to learn about new things.

Word to Know

observe

The Five Senses

You **observe** when you use your senses.
You have five senses.
Your senses are sight, hearing,
smell, touch, and taste.
You can observe color with
your sense of sight.
You can observe size and shape
with your senses of sight and touch.

Underline the sentence that tells
how you observe.

This tree frog lives
in the rainforest.

● **Picture Clues** **Write** one thing you
observe about the frog in the picture.

_____

Observe and Predict

You observe things.

You use what you observe to predict.

Predict means to tell what might happen next.

Suppose you observe that danger is near.

You can predict what the fish will do.

You might predict the fish will swim away.

◉ **Picture Clues** Look at the fish.

Tell about their size, shape, and color.

Predict what this fish will do when it gets hungry.

Compare and Classify

You share what you observe with others.
You compare what you observe.
You can compare how things are alike.
You also talk about how things
are different.

You classify things too.
You classify when you group things
by how they are alike.
You can classify the fish by color.

Tell a partner how the fish are alike.

At-Home Lab

Classify Objects
Gather ten small objects from around your home. Observe the shape of each object. Make a chart to classify the objects by shape.

How do scientists use tools?

Envision It!

Tell how you can use these tools safely.

Inquiry **Explore It!**

Why do scientists use tools?

☑ **1.** Pick an object. Use a metric ruler to **measure** its length in centimeters. **Record.**

☑ **2.** Use paper clips to measure the object. Record its length in paper clips.

Explain Your Results

3. Think about the 2 ways you **measured.** Why might scientists use a metric ruler and not paper clips?

Materials

paper clips

metric ruler

Object Length

Length in centimeters	
Length in paper clips	

I will know how to use some science tools. I will know how to do science safely.

Words to Know

tool   safety

measure

Tools

Scientists use many different tools. A **tool** is something that makes work easier.

You can use tools to observe.

A hand lens is a tool.

A hand lens makes objects look bigger.

A microscope makes objects look bigger too.

You can see small things with a microscope.

You cannot see these things with just your eyes.

hand lens

<u>**Underline**</u> what makes work easier.

Draw an X on the tool that helps you see things you cannot see with just your eyes.

microscope

A **thermometer** measures temperature. Temperature is how hot or cold something is. This thermometer tells temperature in degrees Fahrenheit and Celsius.

Measure with Tools

When you **measure** you learn the size or amount of something.

You use tools to measure.

Sometimes scientists do not measure.

Sometimes scientists estimate. An estimate is a careful guess about the size or amount of something.

(Circle) the tool that measures how hot something is.

A **rain gauge** measures how much rain has fallen.

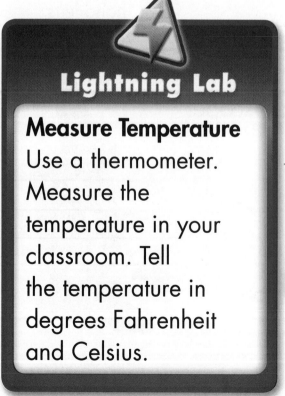

Lightning Lab

Measure Temperature
Use a thermometer. Measure the temperature in your classroom. Tell the temperature in degrees Fahrenheit and Celsius.

A **pan balance** measures how much mass an object has.

A **clock** measures time.

A **measuring cup**
measures volume.
Volume is how much space
something takes up.

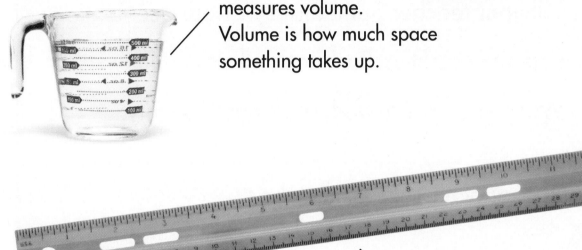

A **ruler** measures how
long something is. This
ruler measures in inches
and centimeters.

Choose a tool to measure how long your shoe is.
Write what it measures in inches and centimeters.

Safety in Science

Safety means staying out of danger.
Follow these safety rules when you do activities.

1. Never taste or smell materials unless told to do so.

2. Keep your workplace neat and clean.

3. Tell your teacher immediately about accidents.

4. Listen to your teacher's instructions.

5. Wash your hands well after each activity.

Write another rule for the chart.

The girl washes her hands with soap and water.

Picture Clues Tell how the girl stays safe.

Tie your hair back if it is long.

Wear safety goggles when needed.

Wear gloves to keep your hands safe.

Handle scissors and other equipment carefully.

Clean up spills immediately.

You spill water on the floor.

Circle the rule that you should follow.

Write why it is important to follow safety rules.

_____

How do scientists find answers?

Envision It!

Tell what the person might want to learn.

Inquiry **Explore It!**

How do scientists answer questions?

Materials

black paper

☑ Think about the following question.

Can sunlight warm an object?

Answer the question as a scientist would.

☑ **1. Observe** a piece of paper. Feel it. It is **(warm/cool).**

☑ **2.** Make a **prediction.**

The paper will get **(warm/cool)** in sunlight.

☑ **3.** Test your prediction. Put the paper in sunlight.

Wait 15 minutes. The paper got **(warm/cool).**

Explain Your Results

4. Draw a Conclusion Can sunlight warm objects? _____

Tell how you know.

Word to Know

investigate

Science Inquiry

You ask questions when you do science.
You investigate to find answers.
To **investigate** is to look for answers to questions.

Scientific methods are a way to investigate.
Scientific methods have many steps.

(Circle) the word that means to look for answers to questions.

This scientist investigates plants.

⊙ **Picture Clues** Look at the picture.
Ask a question the scientist might ask about plants.

Scientific Methods

Ask a question.

Ask a question that you want answered.
How does sunlight change the way plants grow?

Make your hypothesis.

Tell what you think might be the answer to your question.
If a plant is moved away from sunlight, then it will grow toward the sunlight because plants need light.

Plan a fair test.

Change only one thing.
Keep everything else the same.
Move one plant away from the window.

Tell another hypothesis.

Do your test.

Test your hypothesis.

Do your test more than once.

Observe the results of your test.

See if your results are the same.

Collect and record your data.

Keep records of what you find.

Use words or drawings to help.

Draw a conclusion.

Decide if your observations
match your hypothesis.
Tell what you decide.
Compare your conclusion
with a partner's conclusion.

Lightning Lab

Fast Claps
How many times can
you clap your hands
in one minute? Plan a
test with three steps.
Do your test.

The boy draws a picture to
keep records.

⊙ **Picture Clues Write** how sunlight
changes the way plants grow.

Tell how you know.

How do scientists share data?

Write what you observe about the dog.

What are some ways to record and share data?

☐ **1.** Stack the cups as high as you can. Make a tally mark each time you add a cup.

☐ **2. Record** the total using a number.

☐ **3.** Repeat 3 more times.

Explain Your Results

4. Compare data with others. Tell any pattern you find.

5. You **recorded data** in 2 ways. How else could you have recorded data?

Materials

10 paper cups

Trial	Number of Cups	Total
1		
2		
3		
4		

UNLOCK
THE BIG
? I will know how
scientists share the
data they collect.

Data

You collect information when you
do science.
This information is called **data.**
You can use pictures and words
to show what you observe.
You can use numbers too.

⊙ **Picture Clues Draw** the data
that the girl in the picture might draw.

Record Data

You **record** when you write
or draw what you learn.
A chart is a way to record data.

Ask five people if they like a cat, a
dog, or a bird best.
Fill in a square in the chart next to
the animals your classmates choose.

Favorite Animals

cat					
dog					
bird					

At-Home Lab

Favorite Pet Name
Think of three pet
names. Ask six people
which name they like
best. Make a chart to
record their choices.

Show Data

You can use charts to show data.
You can also use graphs.
Use your data to make a
picture graph.

Count the votes for each pet.
Draw one animal for each vote.

Favorite Animals

Pet	1	2	3	4	5
cat					
dog					
bird					

Number of votes

Write a conclusion from your data.

_____

_____

_____

How do you know the mass of objects?

Follow a Procedure

☐ **1. Measure** the mass of a cup.
First, put the cup on one side of a balance.
Next, slowly add gram cubes to the other side.
Then, stop when the balance is level.
Last, **record** the mass on the chart.

☐ **2.** Measure the mass of 10 beans. Record.

☐ **3.** Measure the mass of the cup with the 10 beans inside. Record.

Materials

plastic cup

10 beans

balance

gram cubes

Inquiry Skill Scientists observe what happens and **record** their results.

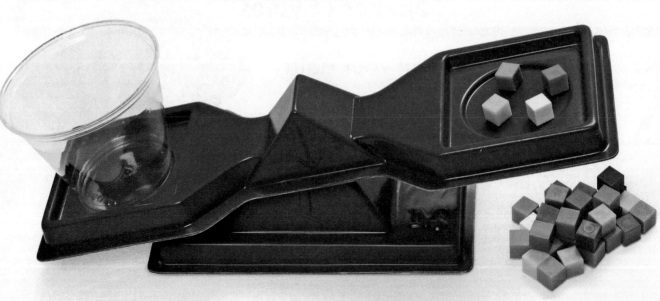

Mass of Objects

Object	Mass (grams)
Cup	
10 beans	
Cup with 10 beans	

Analyze and Conclude

4. Look at your data.
   Add the mass of the cup and the beans.

   _____ grams + _____ grams = _____ grams

   (cup) (beans) (cup with 10 beans)

5. **Draw a Conclusion** Did the cup and beans
   have the same mass together as they did
   separately?

   _____

   _____

   _____

Big World

**BigWorld
My World**
Read Together

Hubble Space Telescope

Look up at the night sky. The stars seem to twinkle. They twinkle because of the air around Earth. The air blocks our clear view of the stars. The Hubble Space Telescope circles above Earth's air. It has a clear view of the stars and other things in space. The telescope sends pictures to Earth. Scientists use the pictures to study space.

My World

Write how the Hubble Space Telescope helps scientists study space.

Vocabulary Smart Cards

inquiry
observe
tool
measure
safety
investigate
data
record

Play a Game!

Cut out the cards.

Work with a partner.

Pick a card.

Act out the word.

Have your partner guess the word.

179

measure

medir

inquiry

indagación

safety

seguridad

observe

observar

investigate

investigar

tool

instrumento

looking for answers

buscar respuestas

to use a tool to find the size or amount of something

usar un instrumento para saber el tamaño o la cantidad de algo

when you use your senses

cuando usas tus sentidos

staying out of danger

estar fuera de peligro

something that makes work easier

algo que hace más fácil el trabajo

to look for answers to questions

buscar respuestas a las preguntas

data

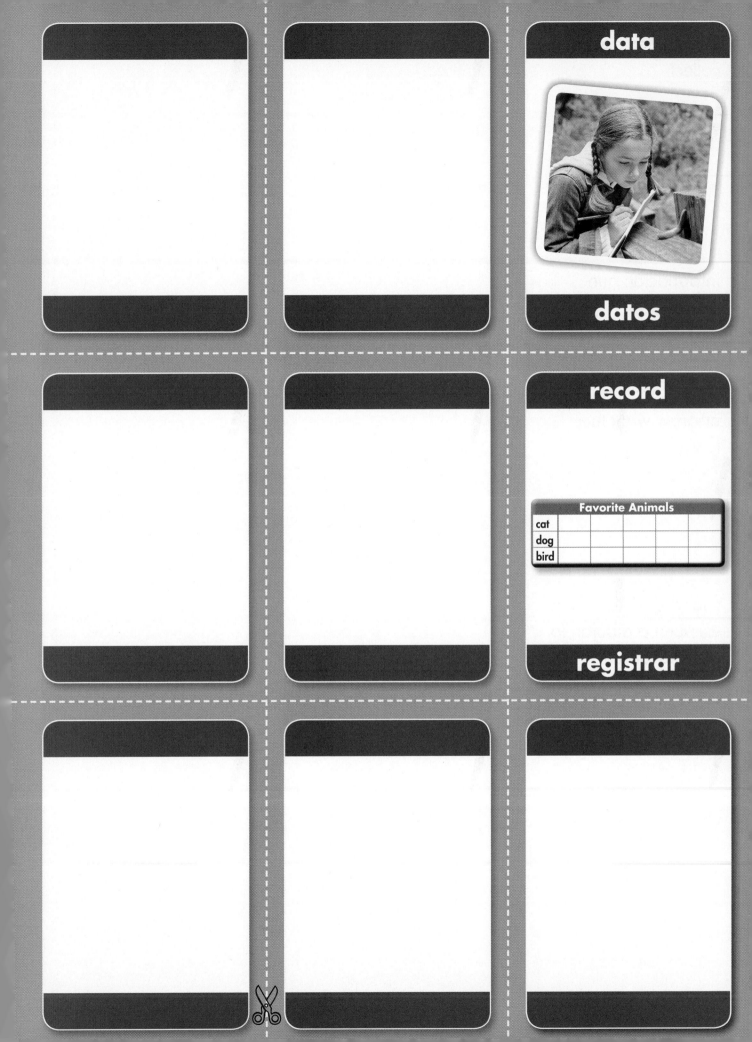

datos

record

Favorite Animals				
cat				
dog				
bird				

registrar

information you
collect

información que
reúnes

when scientists write
or draw what they
learn

cuando los científicos
escriben o dibujan lo
que descubren

Lesson 1

What questions do scientists ask?
- Scientists ask questions about the world.
- Scientists answer questions with inquiry.

Lesson 2

What skills do scientists use?
- Scientists use their senses to observe.
- Your senses help you describe things.

Lesson 3

How do scientists use tools?
- You can use tools to measure objects.
- Always follow safety rules.

Lesson 4

How do scientists find answers?
- Scientists use many methods to investigate.
- Scientists test things many times.

Lesson 5

How do scientists share data?
- Scientists observe and record data.
- You can use charts to record.

Lesson 1

1. Vocabulary What is inquiry?

_____

_____

2. Apply Some scientists ask questions about weather. **Write** a question you have about weather.

_____

_____

_____

Lesson 2

3. Compare (Circle) the scientist who listens to observe.

Lesson 3

◉ **4. Picture Clues** **Write** how the children stay safe.

_____

_____

Lesson 4

5. Vocabulary Write what scientists do when they investigate.

Lesson 5

6. What do scientists use to keep records? **Fill in** the bubble.

Ⓐ words and pictures   Ⓒ safety

Ⓑ tools such as saws   Ⓓ scientific methods

Got it?

⬛ **Stop!** I need help with

▶ **Go!** Now I know

What are they making?

The Design Process

Write what you think they will make.

How do you solve problems?

How can you design a top?

☑ **1.** Make the top in the picture.

Materials

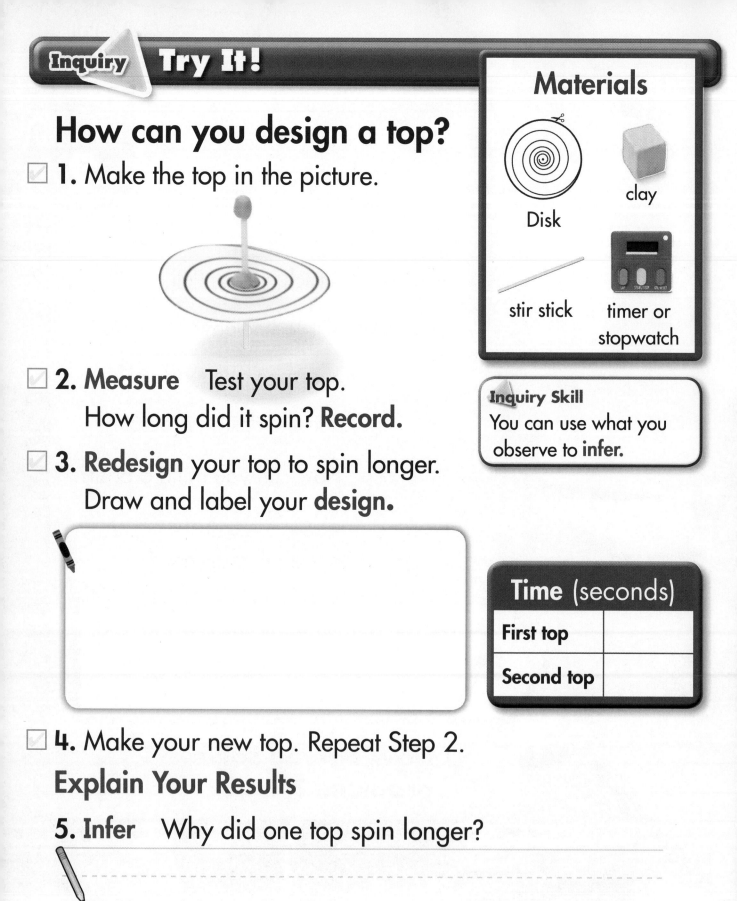

Disk

clay

stir stick

timer or stopwatch

Inquiry Skill
You can use what you observe to **infer.**

☐ **2. Measure** Test your top. How long did it spin? **Record.**

☐ **3. Redesign** your top to spin longer. Draw and label your **design.**

Time (seconds)	
First top	
Second top	

☐ **4.** Make your new top. Repeat Step 2.

Explain Your Results

5. Infer Why did one top spin longer?

_____

_____

_____

⊙ Sequence

Sequence means to tell what happens first, next, and last.

Block Castle

You want to build a block castle.
First, you gather blocks.
Next, you stack the blocks.
Last, you look at your castle.
It is very high!

Practice It!

Write what comes next.

First

I gather blocks.

⬇

Next

_____

⬇

Last

I look at my castle.

Reach, Grab, Pull

Magnets can be different shapes and sizes. Magnets are made of metals. Magnets attract some metals. Magnets can pick up some objects.

It can be hard to reach objects that are far away. You can use magnets to help. You can attach a magnet to the end of a pole. Some metal objects will stick to the magnet. You can pick up the object. You can pull it towards you.

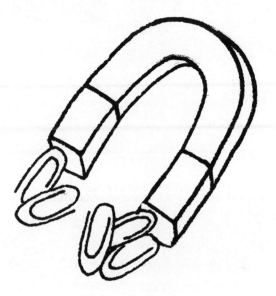

Find out what things magnets attract.

What will you use as a pole to attach your magnet to?

Find a Problem

☑ **1.** You need to reach something that is across the room. Write what you will build.

☑ **2. Draw** what you will build.

Plan and Draw

☑ **3.** What can magnets attract?

☑ **4. Draw** the shape of your magnet.

☑ **5.** Think about how far away your object is. How long will your pole be?

_____

_____

☑ **6.** How will you attach your magnet to your pole?

_____

_____

_____

_____

Choose Materials

Look at the materials. Think about how to attach a magnet to a pole so you can pick something up.

☑ **7.** What could make your design difficult?

_____

_____

_____

☑ **8.** Pick one material you will not use. Write why.

_____

_____

_____

☑ **9. Draw** what your pole and magnet will look like. **Label** all the materials.

Make and Test

☑ **10. Build** your pole and magnet.

☑ **11. Draw** your pole and magnet. Does it look the same as your plan? Does it look different than your plan? Write.

☐ **12.** Use your pole and magnet to pick up the object you chose. Try several times.

☐ **13.** Did your object stick to the magnet? **Circle.**

Yes   **No**

☐ **14.** Did the object stay stuck to the magnet long enough for you to grab it? **Circle.**

Yes   **No**

Record and Share

☑ **15. Compare** your pole and magnet with another. Write how the pole and magnets are the same.

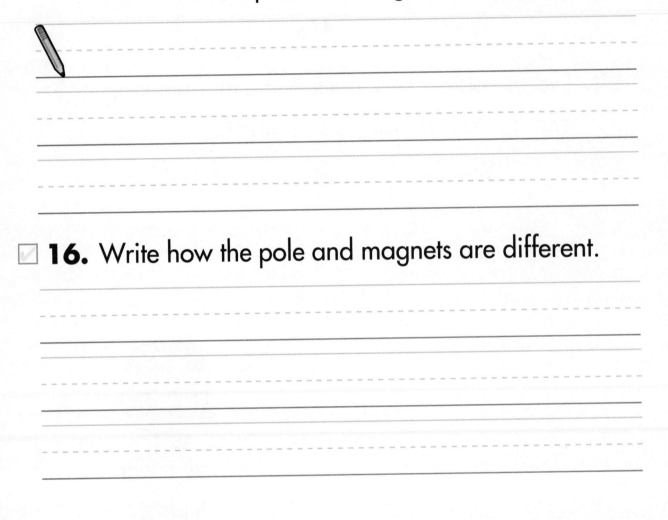

☑ **16.** Write how the pole and magnets are different.

☑ **17.** How can you redesign your pole and magnet?

_____

_____

_____

_____

☑ **18. Draw** your new design.

Lesson 1
What is technology?

Write the parts of the bicycle.
Use words from the list.

Inquiry **Explore It!**

Which tool works better?

☑ **1. Predict** Which tool will pick up cubes better?

☑ **2.** Use each tool to pick up cubes.

Explain Your Results

3. Record What happened when you used each tool?

_____

_____

4. Draw a Conclusion Which tool worked better? Explain.

_____

_____

_____

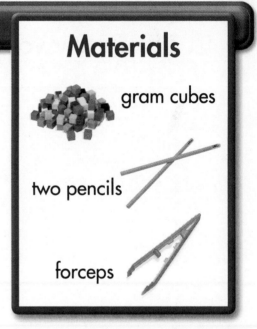

Materials

gram cubes

two pencils

forceps

200

tire
pedal
seat
handlebars

Word to Know

technology

Technology

Bicycles are a kind of technology.
Technology is using science to help
solve problems.

Scientists use technology to
make discoveries.

Sometimes scientists discover
new technology.

Circle the technology the boy is using.

Tell what it is.

Tell what would happen if a bicycle did
not have one of its pedals.

Technology helps
scientists do
their work.

Helping Earth
Think of a technology that helps keep the air or water clean. Tell how it helps.

This boy uses a pencil to communicate. A pencil is technology.

Solve Problems

Technology helps people solve problems.
One problem is that people need to communicate with each other.
They might not be in the same place.
They use a telephone.
A telephone is technology.

Underline a problem that technology solves.

◎ Sequence **Look** at the time line. **Write** what people invented first.

_____

_____

Technology over Time

1870

The first all metal bicycle is invented.

1876

The first telephone call is made.

1946

The first computer is built.

Help People

Technology helps people stay safe.

People use cars to get from place to place.

Seat belts help make cars safe.

Air bags help make cars safe.

Safety seats help keep children safe.

Technology helps keep people safe in cars.

Underline three kinds of technology a car has.

Draw another kind of technology.

Tell how it solves a problem or helps people.

2001

MP3 players become popular.

Draw something you would like to invent.

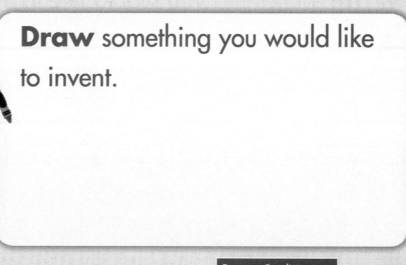

What are objects made of?

Tell three objects that people made.

my planet Diary

DISCOVERY

Read Together

Do you like to eat popcorn? Orville Redenbacher wanted to find the kind of corn that made the best popcorn. He grew many different kinds of popcorn. He tested many kinds of corn. Finally, he found a corn that made good popcorn.

Underline what Orville Redenbacher tested.

Write something you would like to test.

UNLOCK
THE BIG
?
I will know what some objects are made of.

Word to Know
....
natural

Different Materials

Objects are made of materials.

Some materials are natural.

Natural means not made by people.

Materials that come directly from

Earth are natural.

Wood and cotton are natural.

Rocks and minerals are natural too.

Sometimes people use natural

materials to make new materials.

Plastic is a new material people make.

Write one natural material and one

material made by people in the picture.

_____

Natural Materials

Natural materials are different from each other.

They can be used in different ways.
Wood is hard.
People use wood to make buildings.
Cotton is soft.
People use cotton to make clothes.

Circle the kind of material you might use to make a pillow.
Tell why you might use that material.

◉ **Picture Clues**
Write why you think rock is a good material for building a house.

cotton

rock

wood

Human-Made Materials

People make new materials.
These new materials can be used
in different ways.

Plastic is a new material.
Some plastic is hard.
Some plastic is soft.

Some objects are made of more
than one material.
A chair can be made of plastic
and wood.

Write two things that are made
of plastic.

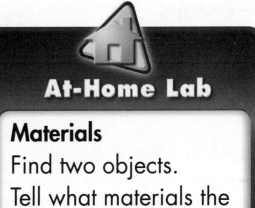

People store food
in plastic containers.

Packing foam is
made by people.

At-Home Lab

Materials
Find two objects.
Tell what materials the
objects are made of.
Tell if the materials are
natural or made by
people.

What is the design process?

Draw a line from the bowl to each object that might be inside.

Inquiry **Explore It!**

Which design works best?

☑ **1.** Pick a bird feeder to build.

☐ **2.** Build it. Put it outside.

☐ **3.** **Observe** for 5 days.
   Record.
   Compare your
   feeder with others.

Explain Your Results

4. Which **design** worked the best?

_____

5. How can you **redesign** your feeder to attract more birds?

_____

Materials

Bird Feeder Chart

Build a Bird Feeder

binder clips

bird feeder food

scissors

string   containers

Words to Know

goal solution

A Problem and a Goal

Wood ducks are animals that need shelter.

This is a problem.

You want to help wood ducks find shelter.

First, you set a goal to design a house for wood ducks.

A **goal** is something you want to do.

Your wood duck house will be a solution.

A **solution** solves a problem.

(Circle) the problem.

<u>Underline</u> the goal.

Wood ducks do not make their own shelter. They use shelters made by people or other animals.

Plan and Draw

Next, you make a plan to build your house for wood ducks.

You write about how to make your house for wood ducks.

You draw what your house for wood ducks will look like.

◉ **Sequence** First, you set a goal.
Write what you will do next.

_____

_____

Draw what your house for wood ducks will look like.

Choose Materials

Next, you decide what materials to use to make your house for wood ducks. You choose something for the walls. You might choose wood. You choose something to hold the walls together. You might choose nails. You need something on the inside so the wood ducks can climb out. You might choose a piece of screen.

(Circle) three things you need to make the house for wood ducks.

tape

wood

screen

nails

microphone

Wood ducks live in many parts of the Midwest and Eastern United States.

Make and Test

Next, you make your house for wood ducks.

You decide where to put it.

You test the house.

You check the house every day.

You see if wood ducks live there.

Write how you know a house for wood ducks works well.

You can share your solution with other people.

Record and Share

You decide how well your solution works.
You plan again to make your solution better.
Next, you record your new plan.
You write and draw to tell about your solution.
You use labels to show parts of your solution.
A label shows what something is.
This helps you remember what you learn.
You can use your solution again.
Last, you can show others how your solution meets your goal.

Label the details of the house for wood ducks.

◉ **Sequence Tell** the sequence you can use to build a house for wood ducks. Use the words first, next, and last.

How can you build a boat?

In this activity you will build a **model** of a boat using foil.

Materials

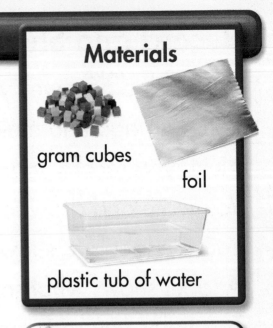

gram cubes

foil

plastic tub of water

Follow a Procedure

☑ **1. Design** a boat that will float. Draw your design.

☑ **2.** Build your boat. Test it in the tub of water.

214

3. Add gram cubes to your boat until it sinks. **Record.**

_____

4. Redesign your boat to hold more cubes. **Predict** how many gram cubes it will hold before it sinks. Record.

_____

_____

5. Test your prediction. Add cubes to your boat until it sinks. Record.

_____

_____

Analyze and Conclude

6. Draw a Conclusion Did your boat hold more or less cubes than your **prediction**?

_____

_____

_____

_____

7. How did you **redesign** your boat to hold more gram cubes?

_____

_____

_____

_____

Trains

When was the last time you rode in a train? Trains are a kind of transportation. Transportation helps us move from place to place.

Technology has changed trains. Engineers design trains. Engineers use technology to make trains move faster. They use technology to make trains safer.

The first trains were powered by steam. Today some bullet trains are powered by electricity. Some trains can travel over 300 kph.

Cars are also a type of transportation. How do you think cars have changed the way we move?

216

Vocabulary Smart Cards

technology
natural
goal
solution

Play a Game!

Cut out the cards.

Work with a partner.

Pick a card.

Show your partner the front of the card.

Have your partner tell what the word means.

solution

solución

technology

tecnología

natural

natural

goal

objetivo

using science to help
solve problems

usar las ciencias para
resolver problemas

something that solves
a problem

algo que resuelve un
problema

not made by people

no hecho por las
personas

something you want
to do

algo que quieres
hacer

Lesson 1

What is technology?
- Technology is any tool that helps people.
- People use technology to solve problems.

Lesson 2

What are objects made of?
- Materials not made by people are natural.
- People use materials for different things.

Lesson 3

What is the design process?
- Something you want to do is a goal.
- You can record your solution with labels.

Lesson 1

1. Vocabulary Put an ✗ on a kind of technology.

2. Apply Technology helps solve problems.
Write a problem you would like to solve.

_____

_____

_____

Lesson 2

3. Sort (Circle) the object with no natural materials.

4. Describe Write an object that has natural materials and materials made by people.

_____

_____

_____

_____

Lesson 3

5. Sequence Write what you do first to solve a problem.

_____

6. How could you test a new ant farm? **Fill in** the bubble.

Ⓐ put food inside   Ⓒ draw the ant farm

Ⓑ tell about the ant farm   Ⓓ see if ants will live there

Got it?

🔲 **Stop!** I need help with _____

_____

_____

▶ **Go!** Now I know _____

_____

_____

What do pill bugs need?

All pets need habitats. A friend gives you pet pill bugs. You must design a habitat for them. What will your pill bugs need?

Find a problem.

☑ **1.** How will you meet each need?

Pill Bug Needs Chart

Need	How I will meet the need.
Air	
Shelter	
Food (energy)	
Water	

Plan and draw.

☑ **2.** List the steps to build the habitat.

_____

_____

_____

_____

_____

_____

_____

☑ **3.** Draw your **design.**
   You will use the materials on the next page.

Choose materials.

☑ **4.** Circle the materials you will use.

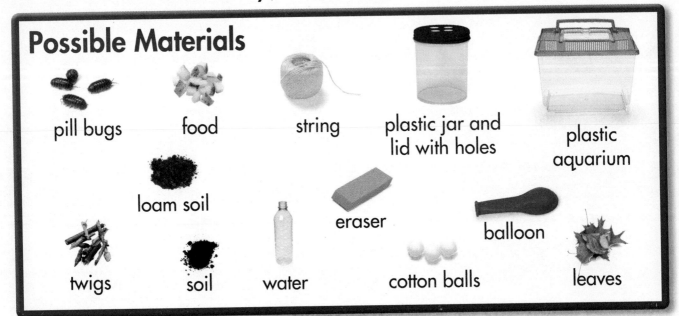

Possible Materials

pill bugs   food   string   plastic jar and
                                lid with holes   plastic
                                                  aquarium

loam soil   eraser   balloon

twigs   soil   water   cotton balls   leaves

☑ **5.** Tell which need each material meets.

Make and test.

☑ **6.** Make the habitat you **designed.**
Follow your plan.

☑ **7.** Draw your pill bugs in the habitat.

Record and share.

☑ **8. Observe** your design for one week.
Observe the habitat.
Observe the pill bugs.

Day Observations	
Day	**Observation**
1	✏
2	
3	
4	
5	

These pill bugs are shown
five times their regular size.

9. Compare your habitat with other groups.
How were the habitats the same?

_____

_____

_____

10. How were the habitats different?

_____

_____

_____

11. How could you **redesign** your pill bug habitat?

_____

_____

_____

Science,
Engineering,
and
Technology

Science and Engineering Practices

1. Ask a question or define a problem.
2. Develop and use models.
3. Plan and carry out investigations.
4. Analyze and interpret data.
5. Use math and computational thinking.
6. Construct explanations or design solutions.
7. Engage in argument from evidence.
8. Obtain, evaluate, and communicate information.

Design a New Hat

- Design a new hat.
- Draw a picture of the hat. Label parts of the hat.
- Tell about your picture.

Write a Poem

- Think of a goal.
- Write a poem about a solution for your goal.

Test Materials

- Draw lines with a pen, a marker, and a crayon.
- Use an eraser to erase your lines.
- Write a sentence about which material erases best.

Measurements

Metric and Customary Measurements

Science uses the metric system to measure things. Metric measurement is used around the world. Here is how different metric measurements compare to customary measurements.

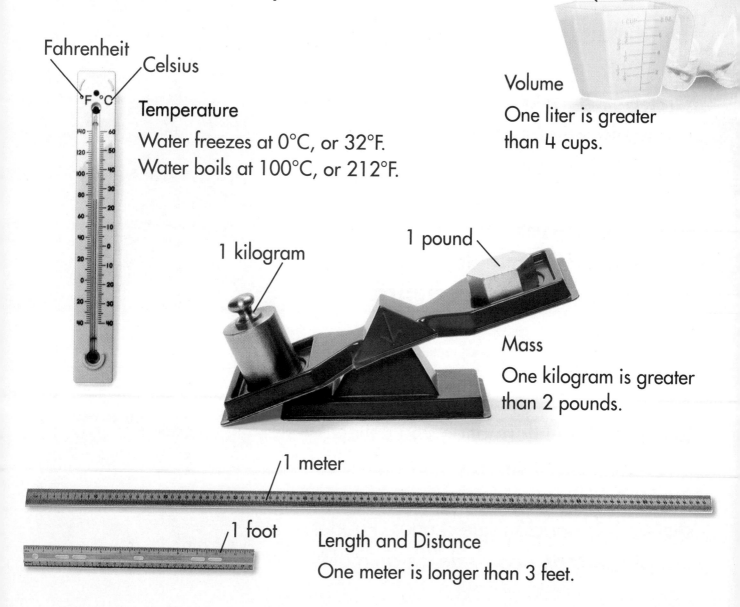

1 liter

1 cup

Volume
One liter is greater than 4 cups.

Fahrenheit

Celsius

Temperature
Water freezes at 0°C, or 32°F.
Water boils at 100°C, or 212°F.

1 kilogram

1 pound

Mass
One kilogram is greater than 2 pounds.

1 meter

1 foot

Length and Distance
One meter is longer than 3 feet.

Glossary

The glossary uses letters and signs to show how words are pronounced. The mark ′ is placed after a syllable with a primary or heavy accent. The mark ′ is placed after a syllable with a secondary or lighter accent.

To hear these vocabulary words and definitions, you can log on to the digital path's Vocabulary Smart Cards.

Pronunciation Key

a in hat	ō in open	sh in she
ā in age	ȯ in all	th in thin
â in care	ô in order	ŦH in then
ä in far	oi in oil	zh in measure
e in let	ou in out	ə = a in about
ē in equal	u in cup	ə = e in taken
ėr in term	u̇ in put	ə = i in pencil
i in it	ü in rule	ə = o in lemon
ī in ice	ch in child	ə = u in circus
o in hot	ng in long	

B

backbone (bak′ bōn′) The set of bones along the middle of the back. A moose has a **backbone.**

columna vertebral Conjunto de huesos a lo largo del centro de la espalda. El alce tiene **columna vertebral.**

D

data (dā′ tə) Information you collect. You can record **data** about animals.

datos Información que reúnes. Puedes anotar **datos** acerca de los animales.

electricity (i lek′ tris′ ə tē) Energy that makes lamps and other things work. The lamp uses **electricity** to work.

electridad Energía que hace que las lámparas y otros objetos funcionen. La lámpara usa **electricidad** para poder funcionar.

energy (en′ ər jē) Something that can cause change or do work. The buildings and the car use **energy.**

energía Algo que puede causar un cambio o hacer que algo funcione. Los edificios y los carros usan **energía.**

goal (gōl) Something you want to do. You have a **goal** to build shelter for the duck.

objetivo Algo que quieres hacer. Tu **objetivo** es construi`r un albergue para el pato.

heat (hēt) Moves from warmer places to cooler places. The **heat** from the flame melts the candles.

calor Se mueve de lugares más cálidos a lugares más fríos. El **calor** de la llama derrite las velas.

herd (hėrd) A group of animals of one kind that stay together. The **herd** of giraffes travels together.

manada Grupo de animales del mismo tipo que están juntos. Las jirafas de esa **manada** viajan juntas.

inquiry (in kwī′ rē) Looking for answers. You can use **inquiry** to learn about kinds of plants.

indagación Buscar respuestas. Puedes hacer una **indagación** para aprender sobre los tipos de plantas.

investigate (in ves′ tə gāt) To look for answers to questions. Scientists **investigate** to learn about plants.

investigar Buscar respuestas a las preguntas. Los científicos **investigan** para saber más sobre las plantas.

L

leaf (lēf) The part of a plant that makes food. A **leaf** fell from the rose bush.

hoja La parte de la planta que produce el alimento. Una **hoja** cayó del rosal de mi jardín.

life cycle (līf sī′ kəl) The way a living thing grows and changes. The **life cycle** of a tree includes a seed, a seedling, and a grown tree.

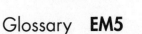

ciclo de vida Manera en que un ser vivo crece y cambia. El **ciclo de vida** de un árbol incluye la semilla, la plántula y el árbol adulto.

M

measure (mezh′ ər) To use a tool to find the size or amount of something. You can use a ruler to **measure** how long something is.

medir Usar un instrumento para saber el tamaño o la cantidad de algo. Puedes usar una regla para **medir** el largo de un objeto.

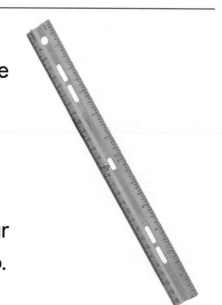

N

natural (nach′ ər əl) Not made by people. Fruit and wood are **natural.**

natural No hecho por las personas. Las frutas y la madera son **naturales.**

nymph (nimf) A kind of young insect. A grasshopper **nymph** does not have wings.

ninfa Tipo de insecto joven. La **ninfa** del saltamontes no tiene alas.

observe (əb sėrv′) When you use your senses. You can **observe** sounds that an animal makes.

observar Cuando usas tus sentidos. Puedes **observar** los sonidos que hace un animal.

parent (per′ ənt) A living thing that has young. The calf needs its parent to take care of it.

progenitor Ser vivo que tiene crías. El becerro necesita que su progenitor lo cuide.

record (ri kôrd′) When scientists write or draw what they learn. It is important to **record** information during experiments.

Favorite Animals				
cat				
dog				
bird				

registrar Cuando los científicos escriben o dibujan lo que descubren. Es importante **registrar** la información durante un experimento.

root (rüt) The part of a plant that takes in water. We covered the **roots** of the rose plant with soil.

raíz La parte de la planta que toma el agua. Cubrimos las **raíces** del rosal con tierra.

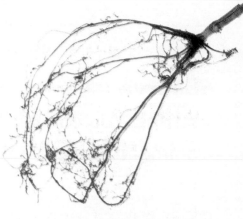

rotation (rō tā′ shən) One spin around. Earth makes one **rotation** each day.

rotación Dar una vuelta sobre sí mismo. La Tierra hace una **rotación** cada día.

S

safety (sāf′ tē) Staying out of danger. The girl washes her hands to stay **safe.**

seguridad Estar fuera de peligro. La niña se lava las manos para mantenerse **segura.**

season (sē′zn) A time of year. Spring is my favorite **season.**

estación Período del año. La primavera es mi **estación** favorita.

seedling (sēd′ ling) A very young plant. Rafe planted the **seedling** of an oak tree.

plántula Planta muy joven. Rafe sembró una **plántula** de roble.

shadow (shad′ō) Dark shape made when something blocks light. The boy made a **shadow** on the ground.

sombra Forma oscura que se forma cuando algo bloquea la luz. El niño produjo una **sombra** en el suelo.

solution (sə lü′ shən) Something that solves a problem. The shelter is a **solution.**

solución Algo que resuelve un problema. El albergue es una **solución.**

stem (stem) The part of a plant that takes water from the roots to the leaves. The rose's **stem** has sharp thorns.

tallo La parte de una planta que lleva el agua de las raíces a las hojas. El **tallo** del rosal tiene espinas afiladas.

sun (sun) A big ball of hot gas. The light from the **sun** warms Earth.

Sol Bola muy grande de gas caliente. La luz del **Sol** calienta la Tierra.

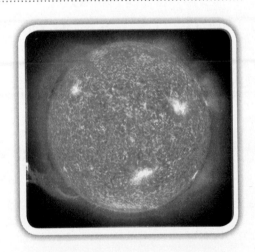

technology (tek nol′ ə jē) Using science to help solve problems. A computer is **technology.**

tecnología Usar las ciencias para resolver problemas. Una computadora es **tecnología.**

tool (tül) Something that makes work easier. A hand lens is a **tool** that helps you see things.

instrumento Algo que hace más fácil el trabajo. Una lupa es un **instrumento** que te ayuda a ver cosas.

V

vibrate (vī′ brāt) To move back and forth very fast. Sound happens when objects **vibrate.**

vibrar Mover hacia delante y hacia atrás muy rápidamente. El sonido se produce cuando los objetos **vibran.**

Index

Helmet, 99
Herd, 83, 84, 89–92, 93
Hubble Space Telescope, 178
Human-made materials, 205, 207
Hypothesis, 170–171

Inches, 165
Infer, 20, 32, 33, 41, 87, 97, 102, 129, 137, 142, 188
Inquiries. *See* Apply It!; At-Home Lab; Explore It!; Go Green; Investigate It!; Lightning Lab; STEM Activity; Try It!
Inquiry, 155, 179–182, 183
Inquiry Skill
  analyze, 33, 87, 129, 177, 215
  ask a question, 40, 96, 136, 169, 174
  classify, 46, 78
  collect data, 41, 86, 87, 97, 102, 137
  communicate, 28, 46, 78, 118
  design, 188, 208, 214
  design your test, 40, 96, 136
  do your test, 41, 97, 137
  draw conclusions, 33, 70, 82, 87, 129, 168, 177, 200, 215
  experiment, 40, 96
  explain your results, 46, 68, 78, 82, 102, 118, 142, 158, 162, 168, 172, 188, 200, 208
  fair test, 136
  infer, 20, 32, 33, 41, 87, 97, 102, 129, 137, 142, 188
  make a model, 128, 214
  make a prediction, 136
  measure, 28, 162, 176, 188
  observe, 4, 46, 68, 78, 82, 87, 102, 118, 128, 142, 158, 168, 208, 226
  plan a fair test, 40, 96, 136
  predict, 40, 68, 96, 160, 168, 200, 214, 215
  record data, 4, 20, 33, 41, 68, 88, 97, 118, 129, 137, 142, 162, 172, 176, 188, 200, 208, 215
  redesign, 188, 208, 215, 227
  tell your conclusion, 41, 97, 137
Insects, 63, 76–77
Investigate, 169, 179–182, 183
Investigate It! 3, 32–33, 45, 86–87, 101, 128–129, 141, 176, 187, 214–215
Irises, 65

Kites, 5

Label, 94, 213
Lamps, 17, 25, 136
Land, 21, 116. *See also* Earth
Leaves, 65, 66, 89–92, 93
  changes in fall, 126
  purpose of, 66
Legs of insects, 63
Let's Read Science! *See* Target Reading Skills
Life cycle, 69, 89–92, 93
  of goats, 72
  of grasshoppers, 76–77
  of plants, 69–71, 98
  of sea turtles, 74–75
Light
  from electricity, 24
  as energy, 25
  on moon, 121
  movement of, 144
  passing through objects, 4, 26, 40–41
  properties of, 26–27
  shadows, 25, 26, 43
  sources of, 25
  from the sun, 103, 114, 116, 119, 121, 122
  types of, 24–27
Light bulbs, 24
Lightning Lab
  Alike and Different, 85
  Bouncing Light, 27
  Fast Claps, 171
  Grow a Plant, 67
  Heat from the Sun, 117
  Make a Plan, 210
  Make Heat, 22
  Measure Temperature, 164
  Science Questions, 156
  The Seasons, 127
Lippershey, Hans, 114
List, 23
Living things, 44–85
  babies and parents, 78, 79–81
  coral, 58
  differences, 83–87
  groups of, 58–59
  needs of, 116
  See also Animals; Plants

Lizard, 80
Look, 103, 202
Loudness, 30

Magnets, 190–199
Make a model, 128, 214
Make and test, 12–13, 54–55, 110–111, 150–151, 196–197, 212, 225
Make a prediction, 136
Make a presentation, 43
Mammals, 62
Match, 62
Materials, 204–207, 211, 224, 228
Measure, 28, 162, 163, 164, 176, 179–182, 183, 188
Measurement, 164–165, 186–187
Measuring cup, 165
Metals, 190
Mice, 96–97
Microscope, 163
Minerals, 205
Mirrors, 27, 144
Models. *See* Make a model
Moon, 119, 120–121, 128-129
Moon calendar, 118
Moose, 62
Moss, 61, 64
MP3 players, 203
Musical instruments, 28
My Planet Diary
  Did You Know? 16, 58, 64
  Discovery, 154, 204
  Fact or Fiction? 72, 124
  Invention, 24, 114

Name, 61, 157
Natural, 205, 217–218, 219
Natural materials, 205–206
Night, 123, 139
Night sky, 114, 120, 128–129, 178
Number, 73
Nutrients, 48
Nymph, 73, 76, 79, 89–92, 93

Credits

Staff Credits

The people who made up the Interactive Science team—representing core design digital and multimedia production services, digital product development, editorial, manufacturing, and production—are listed below.

Geri Amani, Alisa Anderson, Jose Arrendondo, Amy Austin, Lindsay Bellino, Jennifer Berry, Charlie Bink, Bridget Binstock, Holly Blessen, Robin Bobo, Craig Bottomley, Jim Brady, Laura Brancky, Chris Budzisz, Mary Chingwa, Sitha Chhor, Caroline Chung, Margaret Clampitt, Karen Corliss, Brandon Cole, Mitch Coulter, AnnMarie Coyne, Fran Curran, Dana Damiano, Nancy Duffner, Susan Falcon, Amanda Ferguson, David Gall, Mark Geyer, Amy Goodwin, Gerardine Griffin, Chris Haggerty, Laura Hancko, Jericho Hernandez, Autumn Hickenlooper, Guy Huff, George Jacobson, Marian Jones, Abigail Jungreis, Kathi Kalina, Chris Kammer, Sheila Kanitsch, Alyse Kondrat, Mary Kramer, Thea Limpus, Dominique Mariano, Lori McGuire, Melinda Medina, Angelina Mendez, Claudi Mimo, John Moore, Phoebe Novak, Anthony Nuccio, Jeffrey Osier, Rachel Pancare, Dorothy Preston, Julianne Regnier, Charlene Rimsa, Rebecca Roberts, Camille Salerno, Manuel Sanchez, Carol Schmitz, Amanda Seldera, Sheetal Shah, Jeannine Shelton El, Geri Shulman, Greg Sorenson, Samantha Sparkman, Mindy Spelius, Karen Stockwell, Dee Sunday, Dennis Tarwood, Jennie Teece, Lois Teesdale, Michaela Tudela, Oscar Vera, Dave Wade, Melissa Walker, Tom Wickland, James Yagelski, Tim Yetzina, Diane Zimmermann

Illustrations

vi, xv, 3, 37, 39, 43 ©Aleksi Markku/Shutterstock; vii, xii, 45, 93, 95, 99 ©Jens Stolt/Shutterstock; viii, 101, 133, 135, 139 Leonello Calvetti/Getty Images; ix, x, 141, 183, 185, 187, 219, 221, 228 ©James Thew/Shutterstock; 67, 70 Precision Graphics; xv, 88 Alan Barnard; 123, 131, 139, EM8 Henk Dawson

All other illustrations Chandler Digital Art

Photographs

Every effort has been made to secure permission and provide appropriate credit for photographic material. The publisher deeply regrets any omission and pledges to correct errors called to its attention in subsequent editions.

Unless otherwise acknowledged, all photographs are the property of Pearson Education, Inc.

Photo locators denoted as follows: Top (T), Center (C), Bottom (B), Left (L), Right (R), Background (Bkgd)

COVER: George Sanker/Nature Picture Library

FRONT MATTER

i, ii George Sanker/Nature Picture Library; vi (CR) ©Cliff LeSergent/Alamy; vii (CR) Melinda Fawver/Shutterstock; vii (CR) ©JTB Communications, Inc./Alamy Images; ix (CR) ©Radius Images/Alamy; x (CR) ©Masterfile Royalty-Free; xii ©Clem Haagner/Photo Researchers, Inc.; xiii (TC) George Sanker/Nature Picture Library, (CL) ©National Geographic Image Collection/Alamy Royalty Free, (CR,TL) ©Getty Images/Jupiter Royalty Free, (CR,TR) ©Hemis /Alamy Inc., (CR,CR) ©Photononstop/SuperStock, Inc., (CR, BL) James Osmond/Alamy Inc., (CR, BR) Mary Clark; xiv (C, BC) ©Danno3/Shutterstock, (C, TL) ©Multiart/Shutterstock, (C, TC) ©Ulrich Mueller/Shutterstock, (C, Bkgd) Corbis, (C, CR) Roger Dixon/©DK Images, (C, TCR) ©2009fotofriends/Shutterstock, (C, BR) ©Evlakhov Valeriy/Shutterstock, (C, CR) ©Randal Sedler/Shutterstock; xv (TR) ©David Trood/©David Trood, (TC) ©3C Stock/Alamy Inc., (B, TC) ©Daboost/Shutterstock, (B, TR) ©hamurishi/ Shutterstock, (B, TL) ©Sergey Goruppa/Shutterstock; xvi (CL) ©Dennis Hallinan/Alamy Inc., (CR) ©James P. Blair/Getty Royalty Free, (BCR) ©Jupiterimages/Brand X/Alamy Royalty Free, (BR) ©Maridav/Shutterstock; xx-xxi Iriana Shiyan/Fotolia;

CHAPTER 1 ENERGY

2 ©foodfolio/ Alamy Images; 5 ©Blackout Concepts/Alamy; 16 (B) ©Cliff LeSergent/Alamy, (T) ©JG Photography/Alamy; 17 (CR) Thinkstock; 18 (BR) ©ArchMan/Shutterstock, (TR) Ingram Publishing/Thinkstock; 19 (TR) ©Bethany Dawn/©DK Images, (BR) Andy Crawford/©DK Images, (BL) Steve Gorton and Gary Ombler/©DK Images; 20 (T) Ronald van der Beek/Shutterstock; 21 (B) Jupiter Images; 22 (CR) ©Masterfile Royalty-Free; 23 (TR) Jupiter Images; 24 (TR, TL) Jupiter Images, (BR) Library of Congress; 25 (CR) ©iStockphoto, (BR) Noriakimasumoto/Getty Images; 26 (CR) ©Dmitriy Shironosov/Shutterstock; (TR) ©numb/Alamy; (B) The Photolibrary Wales/Alamy; 27 (CR) Thinkstock; 28 (T) Photo 24/Getty Images; 29 (BR) ©Erik Isakson/Getty Images; 30 (BR) ©Jacek Chabraszewski/Shutterstock, (BL) ©Masterfile Royalty-Free, (CR) Thinkstock; 31 (BL) ©Thomas M. Perkins/Shutterstock, (BC) Getty Images, (BR) Jupiter Images; 34 (B) ©Idealink Photography/Alamy, (TR) ©Otmar Smit/Shutterstock; 35 (TL) ©Dmitriy Shironosov/Shutterstock, (CL) ©Erik Isakson/Getty Images, (CR) ©JG Photography/Alamy, (TR) Thinkstock, (BR) Ronald van der Beek/Shutterstock; 37 (B) ©foodfolio/Alamy Images, (BC) iStock International, Inc., (TC) Thinkstock, (T) ©JG Photography/Alamy Royalty Free, (B) Masterfile Royalty-Free; 38 (TC) ©Daboost/Shutterstock, (TR) ©hamurishi/ Shutterstock, (TL) ©Sergey Goruppa/Shutterstock;

CHAPTER 2 PLANTS AND ANIMALS

44 ©Eric Gevaert/ Shutterstock; 47 (BR) ©Regien Paassen/Shutterstock, (TR) Jupiter Images; 58 (TL) ©Al Mueller/Shutterstock, (TR) ©Iliuta Goean/ Shutterstock, (TC) ©Joseph/Shutterstock, (CR) ©Jim Lopez/Shutterstock; 59 (CR) ©Doug Lemke/ Shutterstock, (TR) ©Galushko Sergey/Shutterstock, (BR) ©Kat Mack/Shutterstock, (TL) ©Loo Joo Pheng/Shutterstock; 60 ©Sean Russell/Getty Images; 61 (BL) ©Kent Sorensen/Shutterstock, (R) ©Nadezhda Bolotina/Shutterstock, (CR) ©oriontrail/Shutterstock; 62 (TR) ©G-ZStudio/Shutterstock, (C) ©Hagit Berkovich/ Shutterstock, (B) ©WaterFrame/Alamy Images; 63 (T) ©IRA/ Shutterstock, (BR) ©Ludmila Yilmaz/Shutterstock, (BL) Ingram Publishing/Thinkstock, (BCL) ©Panaglotis Milonas/iStockphoto, (BCR) ©ZTS/